Stitches

Stitches

OFF-THE-WALL TALES
FROM THE DOCTOR'S OFFICE,
HOSPITAL, AND OPERATING ROOM

COMPILED BY DR. JOHN COCKER, M.D.

Published in 1993 by
Stoddart Publishing Co. Limited
34 Lesmill Road
Toronto, Canada
M3B 2T6
(416) 445-3333

Canadian Cataloguing in Publication Data

Cocker, John
Stitches: off-the-wall tales from the doctor's office, hospital, and operating
room

ISBN 0-7737-5605-1

1. Medicine — Humour. 2. Canadian wit and humour (English). * 1. Title

R705.C63 1993   610.207   C93–094501–8

Cover Design: Brant Cowie/ArtPlus Limited
Cover Illustration: Lynn Johnston
Printed and bound in Canada

*Stoddart Publishing gratefully acknowledges the support of the Canada
Council, Ontario Ministry of Culture, Tourism, and Recreation, Ontario Arts
Council, and Ontario Publishing Centre in the development of writing and
publishing in Canada.*

Contents

Preface

●●●●●●●●●●●

The therapeutic benefits of humour have been well
documented. In the Bible you'll find: "A merry heart doeth
good like a medicine" (Proverbs 17:22). And in Norman Cousins's
Anatomy of an Illness we read: "There's not a lot of fun in
medicine, but there's a heck of a lot of medicine in fun."

Thus, when *Punch Digest for Canadian Doctors*, now called
Stitches, first exploded onto the medical scene in Canada, the
acceptance was immediate. The magazine struck a responsive
chord with doctors, nurses, and other medical staffers, and
we've been inundated with jokes, cartoons, and stories ever
since. Needless to say, not all of them have been fit to print.

It seems too much of a good thing to restrict ourselves to
health professionals, so this book is the first attempt to bring
some of the best stories and cartoons to the general public.
Some people may be shocked to discover that physicians have
a sense of humour and can joke about serious matters, but
doctors have always known that humour has no equal in the
relief of stress and the prevention of occupational burnout.

If you have a story to share, or if you would like to subscribe
to *Stitches*, the magazine, please write to us. You might brighten
someone's day, just as we hope we'll brighten yours.

— DR. JOHN COCKER, PUBLISHER

Stitches
14845 Yonge Street, Suite 300
Aurora, Ontario
L4G 6H8

xi

Stitches

PART ONE

At the Hospital

Is There Life After Committee?

■●●●●●●●●●●●●●●●■

The most fundamental decision facing all young doctors at the start of their careers is How to Get on in Medicine. Methods like caring for sick people very well, or superb teaching, are not only old-fashioned but old hat. Today the aspirant has two options: research or administration.

To be successful in research the work must be basic (Electron Microscopy and the Sex Life of the Mitochondrion), experimental (The Effects of Aspirin on Amyloidosis of the Organ of Zuckerkandl in the Chinese Hamster), and vastly expensive — and the successful doctor will end up as an administrator, anyway. Experimentation and writing of papers will be left to graduate students; the researcher will jet around the world, first-class, wearing a blue suit and carrying a leather briefcase with secret combination locks, and deliver the same paper to

"I asked for a blood count on Mr. Westburg — what do you mean there were eight quarts?"

3

international conferences. In between there will be boards and commissions.

Why not shortcut the whole process and become an administrator first?

The initial step is to buy the blue suit and impressive briefcase. The second is to go to meetings, which involves being appointed to committees. And don't forget to wear your new suit and take your briefcase. Never go to a committee meeting in a white coat or, above all, in OR greens. It implies that your priorities are elsewhere.

The primary decision to administer rather than to do is wise for a number of reasons. For one thing, it's a superb career for the merely or below average doctor. Them as can, do; them as can't do, teach; them as can't teach, plan; them as can't plan, administer!

Another point is that administration is never a solitary, lonely activity. Like many other satisfying vices, it's practised in warm rooms, in groups.

With a little careful planning it's possible to spend one's entire life in committee, thus obviating any need for individual thought, action or, most important, individual responsibility. You can be permanently "tied up in committee," rather like a pathologist I once knew whose response to any call for decision-making was: "I'm all tied up with an autopsy!" Quite apart from the Laocoön-like visual image this evoked, of slow strangulation by intestines with a morbid life of their own, it was an effective ploy.

Most committees never decide anything, and it's possible to keep up with their business by attending one meeting in three, which is the speed of progress. This is part of the Green movement, called Conservation of Agendas. Indeed, if committee life is to be exploited to its optimum, the committee never should do or decide anything. It can table, refer, receive, note, amend, debate, and discuss, but forever eschew decision.

There is an inverse relationship between the size of a committee and its decision-making power, first identified by Parkinson in one of his laws, and if the committee is large enough (greater than 23 members), it will never decide anything at all. It is no accident that medical advisory committees are larger than this.

4

The principle is expressed mathematically in Emson's equation, which states that each member contributes Q, a Quotient of Imbecility occupying unit time. No sensible decision can be made until each member has contributed his or her Q; with N members, this occupies N × Q units of time. If this is greater than T, the time available for the meeting, then a sensible decision cannot be reached. If (heaven forbid) you actually want to make a sensible suggestion, it must be deferred until all the other members have contributed their Quotients of Imbecility, or it will fall on deaf ears.

The formula can be refined and applied to each item on the agenda, so that true imbecility applied to the first item, with one member's Q initiating all others, will result in no sensible decision ever being made at all, no matter how much time is available!

The corollary is, beware of small committees. They may actually do something. If the ambitious young doctor conceives a desire to do something, and all self-restraint and appeals to better nature are in vain, then my advice is to try to get appointed as a committee of one, with power to co-opt.

Committee work is rarely hazardous, except to the higher centres of intelligence, which tend to atrophy. On the other hand (if that's the right phrase), steatopygy is a risk.

"As you can see in the monitor, Mr. Stevens, we are now entering your wallet."

*"That bleeping sound you hear is nature's way
of telling us something is wrong."*

Never sit in the same place twice, or the chairperson will learn where to find you. Acquire the capacity to sleep with your eyes and ears open — this should have been learned as a medical student — to avoid being appointed to dangerous subcommittees. Maintain renal function by frequent cups of coffee; trips to the washroom will take care of your phlebothrombosis. Learn the combination of your briefcase — nothing looks worse than a physical attack on the lock — and draw from it yellow legal pads, for constructive doodles, first taking care that your neighbour isn't a psychiatrist, who might diagnose from them. Have all your notes in a ring binder, with filing tabs, and refer to them frequently. If you don't have notes, simulate them with grocery lists, CDs to be bought, or baseball statistics. Write letters to your aunt. Eat — the best committees have lunch.

By looking wise and saying little, you'll attain a great reputation, become chairperson, and report for your committee to the board. Further success can be assured by the use of the latest administrative buzzwords and the circumlocution of a royal commission.

Eventually you'll spend most of your time in Ottawa, sitting on national committees, commissions, and boards. You'll be appointed to the Order of Canada. And, with a bit of luck, you'll become the first medical chairperson of a law reform commission — by that time you'll be indistinguishable from one of them. But you won't notice.

— DR. HARRY EMSON

I Ain't Dead Yet

When I was a first-year medical student, and very early on in first year at that, our clinical group was being instructed on examination skills at the university's Family Medicine Centre. Our clinician would arrange for patients with interesting findings to come in (voluntarily, we hoped) and let us stumble through a history and physical, often with hilarious results. Many of these patients were retired and "glad to be of service" to the "young doctors."

One Monday morning we had a didactic session on cardiac murmurs. Our clinician had taught us how to determine if a murmur was grade IV/VI or worse. I always carried a DeGowan and DeGowan in my black bag, so we looked at the pictures of the kite-shaped diagrams and learned where to listen, where to put our hands, not to breathe on our own stethoscope tubes and think it was a murmur, and other salient advice. We were then turned loose on a patient who we'd been told had "some cardiac findings."

"OK, let's get this straight . . .
she was licking the mixer and you couldn't resist?"

"We still have him on the critical list.
He's critical of the food, the nurses, the bed, the room, and me."

The patient turned out to be a shy 70-year-old widow, who proudly told us it was her first visit "to teach the young doctors." We did our usual attempt at a coherent history, remembering most of a functional inquiry of sorts, and turned our minds over to the examination.

We took a blood pressure in each arm, looked for arcus senilis, tapped her reflexes, and did all the other stuff that one can do with a patient dressed. I then announced that I'd like to examine her heart and could she please lie down for me.

I looked around for a drape or something to cover her but found nothing to use, so she undid a button or two on her blouse so we could slip our stethoscopes in "for a listen." I then leaned on her liver a wee bit to see if her neck veins bulged, and while listening to her heart I realized that for once I actually heard a murmur!

I knew I'd be grilled about the grading of the murmur, and being very excited about actually hearing it, I hastily put my hand on her chest to see if I could feel this murmur through the chest wall.

She looked at me and asked, "What are you checking for, young feller?"

"I'm feeling you for a thrill" was my absentminded reply as I tried to gauge the vibration of the murmur.

She gave me an understanding look, took her blouse completely off, pulled up her bra, and said, "You go ahead and enjoy yourself, young feller. I ain't dead yet myself."

— DR. F. R. SPICER

Lost In Translation

As a medical student-intern in Edmonton, I dealt with a lot of patients who spoke only Ukrainian. One day, trying to be friendly, I used my only two Ukrainian phrases to greet one of these patients.

After I said, "Good morning" and "How are you today?" in Ukrainian, I could only smile and nod when his comments and answers in return were Ukrainian.

As I was leaving the room after all the smiling and agreeing, the patient in the next bed asked if I'd understood what was being said. I confessed that I didn't. He then informed me, "Your patient was asking you if he was going to die soon!"

I quickly left to find a translator to return with me to the bedside!

— DR. ARNOLD DLIN

How I Got into the IV League

A Reminiscence

I stood outside Mr. MacAlear's room in a sweat, my heart rate twice as fast as an elephant's during a mating ritual. I suppose it was a normal heart rate for someone face-to-face with a Bengal tiger, or in a plane at 30,000 feet with the engines on fire. But I was in neither of those situations. I was merely about to insert an intravenous line into a living patient for the first time.

It wasn't going to be brain surgery and it wasn't an emergency. So why were my adrenal glands running overtime, with sweat stains under my arms, a greenish tinge to my complexion, and this damn runaway heart rate? During all those hours in medical school, learning about the blood supply to the left nostril, with its attendant network of nerves, veins, and glands, nobody had told me that one day I'd decompensate totally in front of a patient's room.

By some miracle — I can't remember how — I found myself at Mr. MacAlear's bedside. The words I wanted to say were, "Hello, Mr. MacAlear, you don't know me, but I'm a medical student sent here to put in an intravenous line. The senior resident didn't want to do it because he was too busy with

*"Well, the doctors were right — they said
I'd be out of hospital within a couple of weeks."*

other things, and he gets immense perverted pleasure out of watching medical students toss their breakfast in anticipation of being asked to do this. I've never done this before in my life, but I've watched other people do it a few times. In all fairness, though, I'm probably better at it than your wife, who I just saw leaving your room with her white cane and seeing-eye dog. Please forgive me for what I'm about to do."

Instead, of course, I ended up saying, "Hi, Mr. MacAlear. I've come to put in an intravenous line."

A plain and simple statement. Not terribly informative, but not deceptive, either. Looking back, I guess it was a bit of an understatement.

I wrapped the tourniquet around his arm the way I'd seen it done by others. I quickly discovered that a rubber tourniquet is attracted to arm hair like a bee to honey. I found solace in the fact that the needle was probably going to be painless compared with the agony I'd just inflicted by ripping out the man's arm hair.

I wiped the appropriate spot with an alcohol swab and readied the needle and plastic catheter. I should mention here that Mr. MacAlear's veins were huge. They represented, to a medical student, the proverbial "side of a barn." To miss those veins with the catheter would be tantamount to striking out in baseball to a six-year-old girl throwing a cantaloupe.

But plumbers probably botch the first pipe they solder, and gardeners very likely maim the first bush they trim. Undoubtedly they laugh about those things later, at dinner parties. However, it's an unwritten rule that medical students don't admit to shortcomings like that.

I poised the needle above his skin. I tightened the skin and steadied the vein. More important, I prayed a lot. Really a lot.

The needle pierced his skin and entered the vein — and exited the other side of the vein. I was relieved, at least, that it hadn't exited through the other side of his arm!

Then the vein provided a sight that's familiar to all medical students: it "blew up." The blood leaked out of the two holes I'd made. It became, to be honest, a tiny blue balloon.

"Damn," I said softly under my breath. I took out the catheter and needle and applied pressure to stop the bleeding.

"Is something wrong?" Mr. MacAlear asked.

"No, not at all," I answered, and in that split second I learned what all medical students learn at moments like these. "There's something wrong with the needle." I'd learned to project the blame.

I placed the tourniquet around his other arm. Again he yelled briefly as I plucked those fiendish arm hairs. I cringed sympathetically as my own hairy arms twitched. Again I swabbed the site with alcohol and gently prodded the needle through the skin and vein wall.

This time the angle was right and the needle tip stayed within the vein. I'd done it!

I was dizzy with success. All I could think about was my fellow students.

"A piece of cake," I'd say smugly, soaking up their awe. They didn't have to know about the little blue balloon or the man's now-bald arms.

Revelling in my success, I fumbled to connect the intravenous tubing to Mr. MacAlear and taped it to his arm. I turned to the bottle full of D5W and opened up the valve to start the flow. Then I tidied up, tossed Mr. MacAlear a look that said without words, "I told you I could do it," and left the room.

I was soon to learn about divine punishment for medical-student smugness.

I couldn't wait to relate the whole episode to "the guys" in class later that afternoon. After leaving Mr. MacAlear's room, I embarked on the 10-minute walk to the hospital locker rooms to change out of my lab coat. I headed outdoors and started the climb up the hill to class.

I whistled. I hummed. I was probably grinning from ear to ear.

Then . . . I stopped grinning. I stopped humming. I broke out into a cold sweat that covered by body. Perspiration dripped down the small of my back instantaneously. My pulse went wild.

Had I taken off Mr. MacAlear's tourniquet?

I must have. But did I? I couldn't be sure.

In that instant I mentally retraced every move I'd made after inserting the IV line. In none of those moves did I remember removing the tourniquet. But I must have done it! If not . . . ?

I thought of Mr. MacAlear with tourniquet on — his veins bulging from the pressure, his arm blue . . . and I started running back to the hospital. Faster and more frantically, I ran.

"I didn't realize the bed shortage was so acute."

But . . . if I walked into his room wearing my coat and with sweat pouring off me, he'd think I was an idiot, a world-class moron. On the other hand, if I went to the lockers first and slipped on my lab coat, I'd appear more normal to him and he might not suspect that I truly was a world-class moron. But I'd be wasting time.

No, I realized that I couldn't live with the fact that if I entered in my street clothes, he might tell everyone in the hospital what a sight I was.

I burst through the front door of the hospital and headed for the lockers. Once my lab coat was on, I sped to Mr. MacAlear's room, pausing for an instant outside his door to regain a semblance of composure. Could I make it look as if this was all normal?

Casually I sauntered over to his bed and suppressed every ounce of my alarm when my worst fears were realized. There, above his elbow, was the tourniquet, still in place. His veins were huge, as I'd imagined. Blood, under the pressure of the backflow, had climbed halfway up the intravenous tubing toward the bottle.

My heart raced as I leaned over his bed. I had to look as if I knew what I was doing, I thought. I reached down and snapped the tourniquet open, trying to hide the tremor.

"That should do it," I said to him. There was a very pregnant pause. He didn't look as though he suspected anything extraordinary had happened.

"Thanks, Doc," he said with hesitation. I looked away in embarrassment. And I walked out of his room in shame.

The rest of the day is an unimportant memory. I can recall only two things: the brief moment of triumph as I successfully inserted my first intravenous line, and the mistake that ruined the triumph. Today I can laugh about it, and I like to think that Mr. MacAlear would laugh with me. I still don't know if he ever realized what had really gone on that day.

Sometimes I tell this story to illustrate my early struggle with conceit and excess pride. Most of all, though, I tell it because it's reminiscent of medical school itself: success, smugness, pride, embarrassment, and another lesson learned.

Over the years the number of embarrassing moments has dwindled, and the moments of pride and accomplishment have become more numerous. But I'm always humbled by the memory of my first experience with an intravenous needle.

— DR. MARK MILLER

"It looks as though Mr. Markham has rejected his new heart."

We have instructed our registrars to phone patients on the waiting list to ensure that they have not died without notifying the hospital.

— AMA BRANCH NEWS, MELBOURNE, AUSTRALIA

Patients spend 10 to 16 weeks in hospital from the time they are diagnosed to the time they die. We must get this down to seven to 10 days. Practice nurses can make it happen.

— GENERAL PRACTITIONER

True Confessions

A colleague related the following incident that occurred while he was an intern in the ER.

A young teenage female was admitted to the department complaining of abdominal pain. The attending physician, after the usual barrage of questions, asked her if she was sexually active.

Sheepishly she looked up and replied, "No, I just lie there."

— DR. HOWARD SHIFFMAN

Novel Treatment

A long time ago when I was an intern at a Toronto teaching hospital, a patient came to Emergency with a fish bone stuck in her throat. The ENT staff physician on call was contacted and the intern was told to take the patient to the ENT operating room.

Just outside the Emergency was a corridor with a gently sloping ramp that led to another part of the hospital where the ENT OR was located.

At the top of the ramp the intern lost control of the wheelchair, which hurtled down the ramp. At the bottom of the ramp one of the wheels of the wheelchair caught on the doorway and the patient was thrown to the ground. The patient immediately coughed up the fish bone.

The intern, with great presence of mind, said, "You're awfully lucky, lady. Usually we have to do this two or three times before we get it out."

— DR. JAMES WATT

How to Reduce Medical Costs

An Idea Whose Time Has Come?

It's quite obvious that of all the patients who see their doctors every day in Canada, some don't actually require the skill and knowledge of a physician.

It has been suggested that these patients could more properly be seen by someone with lesser qualifications. As the nursing profession is anxious to muscle in on the prestige accorded to doctors, why not let nurses see these patients? This idea is so excellent that we should follow it through to its logical conclusion, and save the health system some really big money . . .

Of the many patients who will now be seeing nurses instead of physicians, some won't really need a nurse's attention, skill, and experience. Therefore we could save money by having these patients see someone with a smaller amount of training and a lower rate of pay — a nursing assistant.

Similarly, of the patients who would now be seeing nursing assistants, some wouldn't require the undeniable skill and knowledge that nursing assistants have developed over the years. So it would only be sensible if these patients were seen by hospital clerical workers, who have less training and experience and are paid at lower rates.

Similarly, of the patients now being seen by hospital clerical workers, some won't need the degree of skill and training that the clerical workers have, and these could well be seen by hospital cleaners.

The hospital cleaners are paid less, so there should be substantial savings for patients who receive their consultation

16

*"I'm afraid there's been an error,
Mr. Thackley. You've been cured
instead of another patient."*

from the cleaners. But the hospital cleaners will now be spending much of their time seeing patients, which will unfortunately mean they'll have less time available for their other duties. As a result, the hospitals won't be cleaned in a satisfactory manner.

Where can we find a group of people with experience in the health field who could take over the duties of cleaning the hospitals? The answer to this question is clear: physicians have had some of their time freed up, since many of their patients are now being seen by nurses. We therefore propose that physicians use this spare time to take over the duties of the hospital cleaners. In this way everyone remains happily employed. The only problem that remains unsolved is: how do we decide which patients are to be seen by which professionals?

— DR. JOHN COCKER

That's the Word!

It was my second shift in the Emergency Department as a resident when a 17-year-old came in complaining of an unusual rash. In the course of a complete history I asked if she was on any medication, including the birth-control pill. She replied, "No, I'm not on the birth-control pill as I'm trying to get pregnant."

"You were right all
along — you're not overweight,
you're just big-boned."

Later in the interview she commented that she'd recently moved to Calgary from Toronto, and elaborated by saying, "We just moved here because my fiancé was recently castrated."

I was puzzled by this unusual statement, especially with her earlier remark that she was trying to conceive. So I asked, "Do you mean to say that your fiancé has no testicles?"

She paused, smiled, and said, "Perhaps I'm using the wrong term. He was recently in-castrated."

After further discussion, I realized that her fiancé had recently been released from prison following a period of incarceration!

— DR. TONY BRILZ

Just Perfect

A good friend of mine, who was not a doctor, applied for immigration into Canada and submitted himself for the required physical examination. The examining physician was young and obviously a recent medical graduate. As he finished, he explained, with an apology, that he was required to perform a rectal examination. He was as embarrassed at having to do this as my friend was at having to submit to it.

After the exam was over, the physician said, "I'm sorry I had to do that, but you know, only perfect assholes are allowed into Canada!"

— DR. MICHAEL GOLBEY

All's Well That Ends Well

While still a medical student in Saskatchewan, I had occasion to examine a retired farmer who was quite deaf "from the combines." The history and physical were a trial of (his and) my patience, but we persevered to "the end."

"Okay," I bellowed, "now I'm going to *examine your bottom.*"

"Eh?" he replied.

"I'm going to *stick a finger in your bum!*"

I was no match for him. He rolled onto his left side and began to *stick a finger in his bum.*

I tried to summon help, but no one came. After some time spent restraining him — did he think I was trying to help? — he finally tired of it and gave up. I had to leave the room in embarrassment to hide my tears (of laughter).

— DR. DAVID BROOK

A Slip of the Tang

Being fluent in two languages can definitely have its disadvantages, as I found out after returning from medical education in the Netherlands for a rotating internship in Regina in 1978.

Obstetrical rounds consisted of the usual bedside teaching with a weekly Friday afternoon session in the interns' lounge. Most of the interns and the staff man would be present at these meetings to review exceptional cases, answer questions, et cetera. Our first session after beginning the rotating internship consisted of a review of a normal delivery, which was run through with a discussion of various points.

As luck would have it, my turn to answer a question came up just when the baby's head was stuck on the perineum after an hour or more of vigorous pushing with no end of the delivery in sight.

"I'm the anesthetist —
I was run over on my way home from lunch."

"Dr. Reems, what would be your next step?"

After some thought, I said, "In order to extract the baby I'd use a low *tang* [pronounced 'tongue'] application."

To this, the staff man replied, "Dr. Reems, if you're going to use your tongue, you're going to get yourself into a heck of a lot of trouble."

This, of course, had all present rolling on the floor and asking for more beer and pizza.

Tang is the Dutch word for forceps.

— DR. H. W. REEMS

A Case of Sinusitis

Before the final year of studies New Zealand medical students were allocated to work in a variety of hospitals for their summer "vacations." Greater hands-on experience could be found in the small hospitals, and so I was accepted to work for three months in the most northerly hospital in New Zealand.

It was a 200-bed hospital in a rural, almost rustic setting, presided over by an English surgeon superintendent, scion of a sophisticated British family who, rumour had it, arrived on his first day of work dressed in striped pants and carrying a furled umbrella.

20

His New Zealand counterpart was Bill, who doubled as surgeon and occasional anesthetist, not to mention his market gardening enterprise where he took advantage of the subtropical climate to grow flowers for the metropolitan markets. Bill had been known to arrive at the hospital direct from the fields, dressed in rubber boots and shorts.

I was expected to assess and examine all admissions and suggest appropriate treatments, supervised by the family physicians or surgeons. There is always something to be said for having a bit of lead time anticipating the arrival of a patient, but one of Bill's proposed admissions led to abject confusion until the patient finally presented.

"This patient is in a lot of pain," Bill explained to me on the phone. "He's feverish, as well, but I can't decide whether he has ethmoidal sinusitis or a pilonidal abscess."

Without further discussion he finished the phone call, leaving me to try to remember the anatomical locations of these diagnostic possibilities. I'd rather thought that the ethmoidal sinuses were near the bridge of the nose, and a pilonidal sinus in the lower back, but Bill seemed confident with his differential diagnosis.

Enlightenment occurred when the patient presented with his pain, fever, a pilonidal abscess, and a large unwinking eye tattooed on each buttock!

— DR. EWAN PORTER

A Nocturnal Odyssey

My car, a sorely tested, battered Ford with unsprung springs and shell-shocked shocks, used to provide almost all my transportation needs when I practised medicine in rural Saskatchewan. However, on a couple of occasions my faithful steed was unavailable, so I was forced to use alternative modes of transport.

One evening our business manager prevailed upon me to lend him my Ford as his vehicle was *hors de combat,* and he had relatives to pick up at the station in the wee hours of the morning. Everything was peaceful, not an emergency in sight, so I innocently loaned him the car while he jokingly left me his bicycle in return.

As I should have expected, at 2:00 a.m. an urgent call came from the hospital: a maternity case in trouble and in a hurry. I grabbed my clothes, muttering imprecations at the whole birth process in general and the nocturnal version in particular. Stumbling outside, I blinked at the unexpected blank spot in the driveway, until it all came back to me: I'd loaned out the car!

Fumbling around in the dark, I tried to remember where I'd put the bike. Tripping over a wheel and landing on a particularly painful point on the handlebars, I remembered. I mounted the old CCM and wobbled off into the darkness.

Skirting one of the innumerable potholes pocking the gravelled surface, I ended up with my pant cuff caught between the sprocket and chain, jamming the mechanism and hurling me into the aforesaid pothole. Then ensued a considerable struggle to get free of the cursed chain, which finally ended successfully at the cost of a portion of my pant cuff and the remainder of my composure. The process of restoring the chain to the sprocket in semidarkness was a unique experience that fortunately I haven't had to repeat since, especially under the time pressure of an impending parturition.

With hands and pants liberally coated with black grease, your intrepid volocipedist set out once again on his errand of mercy. A fierce bark, a couple of growls, and out of the dark charged my neighbour's hated black Labrador, taking this God-given opportunity to pay me back in spades for the numerous times I'd sent him packing out of our yard. With a fierce tug and rip went my other pant leg, fortunately without any accompanying flesh. However, as part of my pants went one way, all of my equilibrium went the other, and I ended up squelching into the soothing, soft coolness of the bottom of the ditch.

Thoroughly muddied, and feeling an intensity of rage that must have depleted my entire adrenaline storage, I grabbed a handy boulder and hurled it with unprecedented accuracy. Off went the black miscreant, howling into the gloom.

After struggling with the twisted handlebars, getting them at least into functional alignment, I climbed onto the bike and headed off once again. Wobbling along, I was struck by what a sight I must have been — greasy, muddy, and torn — enough to make any self-respecting babe want to crawl back up the birth canal.

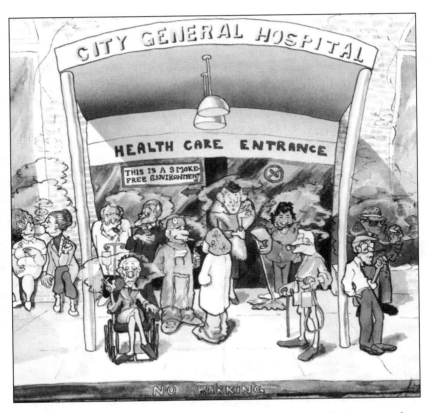

So, I ended up with the giggles and found myself singing a few choruses of "The Last Time I Was Parous (Pregnant), Was in the Early Spring," as I made my way. Fortunately I didn't run into anyone en route, as I probably would have been considered a candidate for the mental hospital in Weyburn. Even more fortunately, there was a hospital back entrance and corridor to the doctors' changing room, where I was definitely able to change for the better!

— DR. BRADLEY HOUSTON

He Swears This Is True!

During a quiet moment on call one Christmas, a colleague related an experience that had occurred exactly a year earlier. A young lady had presented herself at the ER with a gash on her forehead and a rather sheepish grin on her face. On the way to the examining room the nurse had determined that the patient had struck her head on the coffee table, and then had pressed for details.

"It's all rather embarrassing, really," the patient said. "My husband John and I had come to spend Christmas with his sister Cathy here in Inverness, Novia Scotia. He was all tired out, so he went to take a nap on the couch while we were getting supper ready. Anyway, we ran out of poultry seasoning, so I went out to get some more.

"Now, you see, Cathy's full of the devil, right? She took the neck of the turkey and snuck down to the living room, pulled the zipper of John's pants open, and stuck the turkey neck there proud as a flagpole.

"The last thing I remember before coming to was walking through the door, seeing Johnnie sound asleep, and the cat gnawing away at that piece of turkey!"

Honest to God, this is true!

— DR. JOHN LEVINE

Reuse, Recycle?

This incident occurred 50 years ago, but I've never forgotten it, and it was brought back to me by a news item in the Canadian Medical Association Journal, which stated that the Ontario government had released a booklet called *Condom Sense* which, among other things, gives instructions in condom use. I wonder if it covers the following.

I was in the Canadian army in England, serving as a medical officer in an infantry reinforcement unit. The military medical routine at the time of World War II was as follows: the soldier would report to his unit orderly room where the names of all the sick were put on a form with their regimental numbers and age. Then they'd be paraded by a noncommissioned officer to the medical section, where a medical officer would see each in turn, examine and prescribe as necessary, and put the diagnosis and recommendations for disposal on the form.

On this occasion a soldier, who looked no more than 14 years old but whose age was given as 18 (the army minimum), stood in front of my desk and asked, "Please, sir, can I see you privately?"

"And press this button here and the backing changes to an up-tempo rumba."

I signalled to my orderly to close the door and told the young soldier to drop his pants. I must have been a big winner at my regular bridge game the night before to have been in a mood for humour, as the following conversation took place after I noted the typical creamy urethral discharge. Despite the lapse of time, I still recall our talk word-for-word.

"Don't you know what that is?" I asked the soldier.

"Oh *no*, sir! It can't be!"

"Why can't it be? Were you out with a girl?"

"Yes, sir, but I used a safe."

"Are you sure it didn't break?"

"*Oh, no, sir!* I turned it inside out and used it over again!"

To that I had no answer. Certainly the army sex education program appeared to have been lacking. Is the Ontario booklet any better?

— DR. A. J. L. SOLWAY

The Job of Patients

The telephone call came at 5:00 p.m. to tell me that at last the hospital would admit me for surgery. I was due in at noon the next day. That meant a flurry of activity, cancelling patients, giving away precious tickets to a ball game, backing out of an invitation to a dinner and dance at the last minute.

"According to the computer, the waiting room is empty now."

Feelings of relief that I was going to get fixed clashed with frustration at having to drop everything at such short notice. After all, I'd been waiting for months, and the impersonal tone of the call made me feel that I mattered very little in the scheme of things — a feeling I've never really enjoyed.

I was also, beneath a surface of nonchalance, distinctly uneasy. To demonstrate my total faith in the medical profession, I brought my will up-to-date.

Sure, I know how busy hospitals are, and I've spent a good deal of working and learning time in them. But to enter as a patient is to discover a brand-new world that's guaranteed to reduce any ego to a flat zero.

The destruction of your self-image as a significant person begins in the crowded admitting office, where your financial resources are scrutinized, the symbol of your nonbeing, the identity bracelet, is fastened to your wrist, and however well and fit you try to appear, it's presumed that you're incapable of finding your way to your floor: you're under escort. Next, you're divested of your clothes, and thereby of your identity and status.

I learned that the doctors, so recently friends and colleagues, are different when seen through a patient's eyes. They stride purposefully and grimly along the corridors, as if to make it clear that doctoring is a serious business and that laughs are few and far between. Interns concentrate on practising their solemn and wise expressions.

Where were all those friendly guys I used to share jokes with? I realized that I was no longer a person, but a patient.

Nurses, of course, are more visible. I've nothing but admiration for the way they work, but they, too, are apart. Even the cleaners, who pursue their calling with implacable silence and lack of enthusiasm, are somehow separate. The only people that the patient really relates to are other patients.

And that interaction is mostly nonverbal. Each new arrival, at least on the surgical floor to which I was condemned, is greeted with quiet but considerable curiosity.

You quickly discover the problems and peculiarities of the surgical gown, which comes in one size — too big — and is guaranteed to have at least half the tapes, with which it's supposed to be tied, missing. There you are, acutely aware that whatever you may look like from the front, it's not exactly attractive, and from the rear your buttocks are your most prominent feature.

New patients can be easily identified by the speed with which they move up and down the corridors, the protrusion of pajamas or nightgowns below housecoats, and their lack of equipment. Postsurgical patients dispense with pajamas and tend to perambulate slowly in the recovery phase, their legs looking pathetic and skinny beside the strength and rigidity of the IV pole, the staff of life that provides an instant diagnosis of your condition. If things are serious, you may have all kinds of technological miracles hanging from it; as the number of gadgets and bags declines, that, too, will be noticed, with silent envy, by your fellow sufferers.

Pajamas and nightgowns tend to reappear as recovery progresses and the patients, having decided to live, begin to care about their appearance once again.

All these signs are evident to your peers and allow them to assess your condition and rate of recovery during the course of the slow promenade up and down the corridors on the way to health. Once again conversation is minimal, often because it hurts too much; however, a very meaningful "How're you doing?" can be answered by a generic "Coming along" without breaking any patterns of etiquette.

"How're you doing?" is generally asked by a person who's closer to getting out than you, indicating that he or she is now capable of altruistic thought. Of course, you can't reply, "Fine, thank you," because you obviously aren't and, anyway, you need all your concentration just to walk. So, "Coming along," accompanied by the standard wince and brave smile, is a useful technique.

It's a good idea to keep your conversations brief, since there are always a few patients who manage to maintain an air of cheery extroversion, even under such trying circumstances. You should be suspicious of such bonhomie, particularly if it leads to the apparently innocent question, "Who's your doctor?"

This question is rhetorical at best. Its real purpose is to lead you into a discussion of the questioner's own doctor, and then to his or her entire case history. Make up a name, or claim you don't know who your doctor is. And don't let it be known that you're a doctor yourself, or you'll never get away. Use your imagination: say you're a septic-tank cleaner, brothel owner, drug dealer, or even stockbroker.

Should all else fail, be prepared to be very rude, or suffer a relapse into acute pain. Vomiting is a good defence, too.

On returning home from my hospital adventure for the convalescent period, which turned out to last just a week, I had the thought that every physician in training should spend at least two weeks as an in-patient in a large hospital, preferably

"His methods are unorthodox, but he gets results."

for some kind of surgery. The particular problem could be invented by the student, and success in fooling the medical staff — and especially tricking the surgeon into performing the procedure — could be counted positively in final grades.

To experience the powerlessness and helplessness of the patient society and to discover that it, too, has its forms and communications could be a valuable learning experience.

— MARK EVESON

Survival Tactics for the Hospital Physician

Despite intense media coverage of environmental issues, many readers may not be aware that the working hospital physician is an endangered species. There are several predators picking off stragglers in our profession, but the basic threat comes from administrators who hold to the axiom that hospitals operate better without patients and without doctors.

Parkinson's Second Law states that any institution that has more than 500 employees can generate sufficient internal problems to keep itself busy: it no longer requires outside problems. Once that Rubicon is reached in a hospital, someone begins to rationalize services, with the bottom line being that the organization starts to insist that no physician be allowed to interrupt the even frenzy of bean counting.

Clearly it's necessary for the doc to develop certain survival techniques — a physician's *vade mecum* — to remain extant in the hospital. For this I suggest a basic library: *How to Lie with Statistics, The Gentle Art of Verbal Self-Defense, Body Language,* and *The Insult Dictionary.*

The book on statistics is mandatory. You'll soon come to realize that, when faced with a fiat from those who control your destiny on the basis of certain numerical evidence, your best life preserver is a statistical lie!

Simple authoritative data, such as the recent finding that the average Canadian adult possesses one testicle and one breast, can leave a board committee aghast long enough for you to have your wishes approved. "Type II" errors can be used to confound voracious vice presidents as they howl for decreased OR time.

In the process of learning your stats and a little more about hospital administration, you'll be faced with many acronyms. It's vital that you be able to roll ALS, NUA, Q reports, et cetera, off your tongue with the rest of the club. One secret acronym that you may not recognize is YOAD. It stands for You're Only a Doctor. The YOAD syndrome underlies most health-care discussions. An example: how much does it cost to replace a hip? You can calculate this from the amount of time and number of staff involved in this simple procedure. But then you run into the YOAD syndrome: poor doctor, you obviously haven't taken into consideration the high cost of cleaners, the cafeteria shortfall, or the price of a 25-year service award. All of this graphically demonstrates your total incapacity to understand the real cost of replacing a hip — or running a modern hospital. All of which is to be expected — YOAD.

A third rule — very important — is this: always go to committee meetings. Attend as many as you can. Look at each meeting as a deposit in the bank of health. Yes, they're boring and a waste of valuable time. However, committees are the fibre of the hospital industry: somebody has an idea in the committee and it ascends irresistibly to the president.

This is an extreme example of process over outcome. It doesn't really matter how useless or invalid the idea is; as long as it goes through due process, from one committee to another, it will eventually become law. Your only way to have a voice is to be on the ground-floor committee.

Incidentally, reading the minutes of your committee before the meeting begins allows you to terrorize the chairperson, confound the empire builders, and dismay the YOADers. Remember, in committee it's never enough to go for the jugular. Jugulars are protected these days. Your primary objective should be the cremasterics or equivalents.

One virus that can be checked in committee is the plague of administrative ooze, which is the phenomenon whereby once a space is identified as "available," clerical projects will ooze into that area, denying any clinical use. I've observed whole quarters in hospitals engulfed by this osmotic process, which is reminiscent of a Hollywood horror film. Even though patient care areas may resemble the Black Hole of Calcutta (and I remind you that a doctor was the head of the group put into that dungeon), administration will continue to snaffle all the good territory.

It's normal for physicians to be proactive in working for a better life for their patients. It's a strange irony that you have to fight for the welfare of your patients in an institution that claims to be devoted to their care. But such is reality.

Considerable leverage can be gained in this continuing strife if you make a foray into the administrative field. Why not use the current concern about the environment to your benefit? Query your chief executive officer about what's being done about the hospital environment. What happens to discarded plastics? Have we an adequate paper retrieval system that recycles the multiple copies of notices advising us of the resignation of a nursing unit administrator? Is the health training of patients being torpedoed by the incessant flow of coffee that's poured into waiting out-patients?

Finally, never forget that the rule in this hospital business is that health is too important to be left to the doctors; we, the administrators, should be taking it over.

Computers can be programmed to make the diagnoses. Protocols determine the path of therapy. Quality assurance committees ensure that the requisite papers are signed. In this healing Utopia, who needs doctors?

— DR. CHARLES GODFREY

Young and Wrinkled

I recall one evening when, as a keen young pediatric resident, during my Emergency Room rotation, I met Billy. He was a gorgeous four-year-old boy, brought in by his mother during an acute asthmatic attack.

He settled down easily with a Ventolin mask but appeared reluctant to leave the examining room once I'd reassessed him and assured him that he would be fine.

He looked at his mother and pleaded, "Please, can I ask her, can I?"

His mother sighed and said to me, "I'm really sorry, Doctor. I know you're busy, but Billy refuses to leave here until he can ask you about something else. Do you have a minute?"

"Sure," I said, and sat beside Billy to talk with him.

"Well," he started, "it's about . . . my penis."

His mother told me he'd been looking at it, touching it, talking about it almost all the time lately, worrying that something was wrong.

"Yes?" I prompted him.

"Well . . . " He screwed up his face. "It's wrinkled. Just like Grandpa's face, but it's not old. Is it going to be okay?"

Wow, I thought, we sure haven't covered this topic yet in the seminars! Thinking quickly, I gave it my best attempt. "Well, Billy, it's just like the rest of your body. Just as your arms and your legs are going to grow, so will your penis, and it will grow into your skin so it won't be so wrinkled."

"Oh, I get it. So it's okay. Thanks, Doctor." Billy appeared relieved. I couldn't believe it: it seemed so simple, but I guess it worked.

"Thanks," added his mother. "You'd never believe how worried he's been. Now, Billy, you're sure you understand and won't be upset anymore?"

"Sure," he piped up, "I understand. My penis is going to grow as big as my arm."

My mouth dropped open, but I recovered quickly. Billy's mother and I stopped laughing shortly thereafter. As I wiped away a tear, she opened the door to leave and said, "Too bad you only see children. Once I tell my husband, I bet he'd like to talk to you, too."

— DR. M. GAUTAM

"We've run out of lab rats, Henderson —
put this on and come with us."

Clothes Make the Doctor

Back in my time as an intern in the 1950s, part of the persona we liked to project was to look good. I fondly remember polishing my white bucks before showering and donning a newly ironed uniform so that I could feel like the grandest tiger in the hospital jungle. A stethoscope modestly stuck in a back pocket and a Parker fountain pen in my shirt completed the picture.

The stethoscope has come out of the pocket, and current fashion dictates that it must be draped around the nape of the neck. Many of today's residents and interns seem content to wear an outrageous variety of street clothes covered by a lab coat. The pockets of these coats are generally laden down with an assortment of plastic slide rules, SI conversion charts, and handbooks.

Imagine the guffaws today if one of these people showed up in a recently polished pair of white shoes. Now *de rigueur* in footwear is a pair of beat-up running shoes, the more worn and dirty the better.

The great equalizer of my generation — and today's — is the OR greens. Once the interns leave all their trappings in the change room, they're on their own. Hoods, snoods, disposable filter masks, and sheer bouffant caps now replace the dinky little green hats and masks of yesteryear. Only one of my classmates had a moustache, a tiny grey affair that was easily concealed by the OR mask but otherwise too small for him to hide behind.

When I was a child, my doctor attended me in the middle of the night attired as one might expect to see him at high noon — in suit, shirt, and necktie. I'm not sure about the spats. A professional was expected to look like a gentleman. No casual jeans and open shirt then. Even in moments set aside for recreation, the doctor was always properly dressed.

During a year as a general practitioner, I, too, wore a tie day and night. This concession to convention during business hours continues today. Even as a young man attending the rare underground mining accident, I always wore proper clothes, even though they were covered by a jumpsuit provided by the coal company.

"Look, a hospital owning a funeral home is not a conflict of interest. It's vertical integration."

The thought of a jumpsuit jolts my consciousness to a later time when my wife crafted me a blue double-knit polyester jumpsuit, which I proudly wore one Sunday while making hospital rounds. Even without a cravat, I imagined myself as something of a dandy, until I was met by Miss McGlashan, the charge nurse on 3 South.

Miss McGlashan and I had traded banter over the years. She took one look at me in my resplendent outfit and was seized by an uncontrollable spasm of laughter that continued long after I retreated from the ward.

What a rude shock! Instead of starting a new trend, I was the object of amusement bordering on scorn. It wasn't my style to be so decried, so I had little alternative but to go home and hang up the suit in the back of the closet next to the Nehru jacket, also made by my wife and also worn just once.

During my residency, I tried, on a limited budget, to keep abreast of the style of the day. A colleague of mine, an Australian, had a total disregard for fashion. To John Griffith clothes were utilitarian: they retained body heat and a semblance of modesty, nothing more.

One day in the gynecological clinic, John was examining a patient in the left lateral position when I noticed that the only tie to which he could claim possession was becoming enmeshed in the examination process.

"John! John!" I whispered. "Your tie is in the perineum."

"Don't worry, mate," he replied. "It's been there lots of times before."

Twenty-seven years later, when he was on a visit to Canada, I noted that he finally had a new tie, but his best trousers were still peppered with cigarette burns in the same old places. Although still oblivious to the world of fashion, he'd lost none of his charm or goodwill.

Over the years I've learned to relax sufficiently to allow myself the luxury of attending obstetrical deliveries at night dressed in more casual clothes, and have fine-tuned the art of getting dressed in the dark once my sleep has been interrupted by the ringing phone. (That bloody phone has interrupted other activities a lot more important than sleep.)

Usually when I go to bed I doff my shirt and sweater in a single motion so that if I have to dash to the hospital I can simply reverse the process. I feel pretty silly when the nurses point out that my V-neck sweater and open shirt are both on back-to-front. What they don't know is that sometimes my underwear is also back-to-front or, even worse, inside out. I hate that!

"Mrs. Dumpty, we did everything
we could. We had 20 or
30 men in there, and about 15
horses . . . I'm sorry."

Recently, attending a middle-of-the-night delivery, I breathlessly arrived as an intern was conducting what was almost a precipitate delivery. I apologized to the patient, explaining that my dishevelled appearance and casual dress were due to my haste to get there in time.

"Yes, I can tell," she replied. "You didn't do your fly up, either." Times have indeed changed.

— DR. KEVIN TOMPKINS

The Foreign Lesion

I was in the midst of my final-year medical exams in 1949. Never one to take exams with equanimity, I was busy cramming for the writtens and spending hours at the bedside of patients, fine-tuning my ear to recognize various chest sounds and murmurs, for the clinical exams.

Now it was dinnertime and I began to feel excruciating thoracic back pain. In desperation and alarm I contacted my much older brother, who was a successful, busy general practitioner. He was kind enough to come and see me as soon as he could.

He decided a chest X ray was indicated. Since he realized how squeezed I was for time, as this was the week of my exams, he would make special efforts to get the film done that very evening — to my immense gratitude.

He had a favourite radiologist who would have done him this special favour without hesitation, but the man was out of town. He then telephoned several of the younger men who had private radiological practices and finally found one, a recent graduate, who was ready to oblige.

We met in the radiologist's office at 9:00 p.m. There was, of course, no one else there. He turned on the lights, made his preparations, and took the film himself. My brother and I chatted while the radiologist did the developing. My mind remained focused on my exams, the review that still had to be done, et cetera, but I nevertheless carried on an aimless chitchat.

Finally the moment of truth! The radiologist called my brother over, and they spoke in ominous hushed tones. (In retrospect I realized they were probably discussing who would

37

give me the bad news.) Then they approached me. My brother appeared in shock, and the young radiologist apparently felt constrained to assume the fraternal and medical role.

"You have tuberculosis! You'll have to go to a sanatorium!" he pronounced succinctly.

There was a typical small round lesion in the apex of my right lung. I thought to myself — with admirable denial — How interesting! This will be very useful for my clinical exams. It was as if they were showing me someone else's X ray, and I felt a kind of perverse gratitude for their taking the trouble to demonstrate a typical tubercular lesion. My mind remained focused on the approaching exams . . .

July 1 and the supposed beginning of my rotating internship at the Queen Mary Veterans' Hospital in Montreal was fast approaching. I had to inform the authorities that the next year was slated to be spent in the sanatorium in Ste-Agathe.

I arrived at the hospital and wended my way to the Radiology Department, where I met Wolfe Light, then a young radiologist. Quickly I poured out my soulful story.

"Bring me the film" was his curt rejoinder.

Soon I was back with the fateful film. Before even really viewing it, he held the film horizontally, played with it a little, and let out a loud "Harrumph!" He then placed it in the viewer.

"I thought so," he said sternly. Dismissing me, as if this happened every day, he pronounced, "Your TB lesion is a thumbprint." He turned to other tasks before I could even express my thanks.

Now let me confess: although I was greatly relieved, I felt a nuance of masochistic regret. Everything and every situation in life is marked by some degree of ambivalence. I'd read Thomas Mann's *The Magic Mountain* the previous year and had been very much intrigued. I felt I was missing out on a most interesting and perhaps romantic experience — but let's face it, I really preferred knowing about it only in fantasy.

It transpired later that my brother, who had a deserved reputation as an excellent diagnostician, had had his doubts about the assured, though regrettable, diagnostic conclusion of the young radiologist, but how can one argue with a fresh, wet X-ray film?

"Sheer emotional blackmail, if you ask me."

"What a night! I'm not positive, but I think there was one born every minute!"

I had numerous contacts with the radiologist over the following years. Now it was his turn to use the God-given defences of denial and suppression. There was never the slightest allusion by him to this episode. It was as if it had never happened!

There are lessons to be learned from every dramatic episode. I learned (especially during the following internship year) to avoid bending over patients in bed for too long, and to protect my fragile back. I believe my brother learned to be less inclined to get involved in any way with the treatment of family members. Finally the radiologist learned — and this I can only assume — to leave the development of film to the technician and, at least, how to diagnose his own, or anyone else's, thumbprint!

— DR. SIDNEY BARZA

Out of Body or Out of Mind?

R **emember the old lines,** "He's at death's door. Let's hope they pull him through"? Something happened to me once that was pretty much like that.

It was way back in the dark forties when I lived in England and was ordered to serve king and country. At that time I had no remaining martial ambition and wished to remain as anonymous as possible — always the best defence against oppression (never let them find out your name). When asked if I wished to apply to be an officer and a gentleman, I replied that I'd rather do something useful. This answer proved to be something of a tactical error and resulted in my being trained as a mechanic and sent to an antiaircraft unit to service its vehicles.

This posting had some merit. First, I'd be unlikely ever to be killed or missing in action and, second, it was only 60 miles from my parents' house, and I managed, by foul means rather than fair, to spend most weekends indulging in such unmilitary luxuries as baths, hot water, and sheets.

The posting was known as a "cushy" one and so was my job, which was to inspect every vehicle coming in for repair and retest it when the work was done. This meant I could drive around the countryside unchallenged by the military police and therefore could act as transport for the flourishing black market trade in surplus equipment, especially American parts, for which there was a strong demand in local garages.

The work was not only easy but financially rewarding, as well, allowing a standard of living well beyond the reach of other, more honest patriots. Life was not that bad!

All good things come to an end, however, as we all find out. One day, while driving around a corner in a heavy truck, I leaned out of the window to call to a friend and my head hit a tree at about 20 miles per hour.

At least that's what they said happened. Retrograde amnesia dictated that my last memory was of planning the seduction of

41

a nurse on the forthcoming weekend when, bingo, I woke up in a strange hospital where apparently I'd lain for three days.

Not only was the place strange, but I can tell you I was strange, too. I had no idea who I was or indeed what I was, although I was vaguely aware that they were putting me into different ambulances and moving me around the country. Later I found out that I'd been in three different hospitals before arriving at the military hospital in Aldershot, where the ward looked like a vaulted cathedral.

There I was diagnosed as having various fractures of the jaw and skull, but the information meant nothing to me. I'd discovered who I was and was quite happy with my identity. I was Ezekiel and could do some wonderful things.

I could, for instance, do standing somersaults up and down the ward or cathedral — I wasn't sure which — with no effort at all, and could also leap to the ceiling and stay there with no regard for gravity. I had no awareness of pain, only the slight prick of the needle when more morphine went in, and that seemed delightfully often.

The experience then shifted to a strongly illuminated scene in which it seemed that all my ancestors were waiting for me to join them. The feeling was one of great peace and love. There seemed to be some kind of figure beckoning to me; all I had to do was go. Using my newfound powers, I drifted up to the ceiling.

Then the sound of voices caught my attention. Looking back from the ceiling, I saw two orderlies talking beside my bed, where I could see myself lying. One of them was saying, "We always put the ones that are going in the bed at the end. It's less trouble when we take the body out."

I was profoundly disturbed by this statement. They had decided I was going to die! This made me very angry.

"Who the hell do you think you are?" I roared from the roof. I'd certainly show them! I waved goodbye to all those beautiful people up there and returned to my body, and for the first time I felt a lot of pain.

To say that I lived to tell the tale is obvious from the fact that I'm telling it. In a couple of days I was transferred again to a head injury unit, where a lot of good people spent a lot of time making me look like me again, but that's another story.

"No doubt about it, Sarge — animal-rights activists.
Looks as if they made a clean getaway."

I've never speculated on the meaning of all that happened, but I'm sure of one thing. If I hadn't overheard those pessimistic bastards talking near my apparently unconscious body, I wouldn't have lived through that night. I've also been left with the feeling that dying might not be as bad as we've been given to believe.

Up until now, that miserable son of a bitch of an orderly has given me 41 years of high-quality life, and I suppose I should be grateful to him. But to tell you the truth, he still makes me angry!

— MARK EVESON

Giggling Nurses

It never ceases to amaze me that protective amnesia is such an integral part of human life. There's no other explanation for the fact that we're not all single children than the existence of protective amnesia for the process of childbirth.

"That's right. We've moved Mr. Robinson from the intensive care unit to the intensive, no-one-gives-a damn unit."

Surely this is also the reason we all remember events of internship and residency so fondly. The harrowingly long hours and confusing mixture of drudgery and sheer panic that occurred while caring for hospital in-patients seem to fade from memory.

My memories of the most demanding rotation of my residency training, the Intensive Care Unit, boil down to just a few events that still manage to bring a smile to my face.

One example is the Halloween night the ICU nurses decided to retaliate for my showing up to work dressed as a nurse. I was lured into the back corner of the ICU by a fake "CODE," then drenched in IV fluid, anointed with baby powder, and strapped into a wheelchair on an elevator with the buttons pushed for all 12 floors. Such is the level of comic relief needed to deal with the pressures of intensive care.

Rounds on the unit usually consisted of the staff physician, senior medical resident, junior residents, interns, and nursing staff clustered around the bedside of some poor individual with tubes running in and out of every orifice, as well as other entry ports chosen by the attending physicians. Occasionally there would be a family member interspersed among the bedside paraphernalia. Such was the case with Mr. Smith.

Poor Mr. Smith had suffered a stroke the previous night. Although he was comatose, his dutiful and caring wife was at his side. Communicating his condition to the staff physician during rounds, with Mrs. Smith in attendance, took a great deal of tact.

I had tried to avoid invading one of Mr. Smith's few remaining orifices by using a condom catheter in lieu of an indwelling catheter, but could not adequately monitor fluid status as we just didn't have a small enough condom catheter. The one we were using kept falling off.

In what I felt was the most diplomatic manner, I explained, "Due to the inadequate volume of penile tissue we were unable to keep the catheter on and therefore lost track of urinary output."

Mrs. Smith willingly pitched in with, "Oh, well, dear, that's because he has arthritis of the penis."

Not being one to pass up an opportunity, I muttered to the nurse beside me, "I bet that's what he told her when it was stiff in the mornings."

The nurse beat a hasty retreat to get rid of an acute attack of the giggles, and the rounds continued to the next bedside.

— DR. CAROLYN LANE

PART TWO

At the Doctor's Office

Mumblechucks and Snigglypoofs

Have You Ever Had One of Those Days?

I was beginning to feel uncomfortable as Mrs. Mumblechuck kept staring at me. "I'm sure you understand, *Doctor*," she said, emphasizing the last word in a way that seemed threatening. I looked at her blankly, puzzled about what she was trying to get at. I was puzzled, too, that she was back in one of my exam rooms only a day after I diagnosed and initiated treatment for her urinary tract infection.

In silence she reached ominously into her purse and pulled out a bottleful of pills. Then it dawned on me.

"I'm sorry, Mrs. Mumblechuck. I know they're very expensive, but you have so many allergies to antibiotics there wasn't a lot of choice."

"Oh, it's not the cost, *Doctor*." Again that caveat in the way she said the last word.

"We think he swallowed the cell phone."

49

There was dramatic pause as Mrs. Mumblechuck drew in a deep breath. "You know I'm on the birth-control pill?" Another pause. "You gave it to me." Her tone was becoming aggressive; I felt contraceptively threatened. She rose to her feet, dumped the bottle of pills into my hand, and turned to march from the room. At the door she delivered her final sally: "I'm glad I've got a neighbour who knows about such things. It was Hilda that told me not to take them." And, with that, she was gone.

I looked at the bottle. "Pelkanitracin," said the label. One of the newer antibiotics, perfect for urinary tract infections, the rep had said. I got the PDR and found the right page. And there, staring at me from a black-bordered box, were the warning words: "Do not use if the patient is taking any form of hormonal therapy, including oral contraceptive medication." I read the list of side effects that might be expected should one ignore this warning: "Alopecia; dermatitis; gingivitis; liver failure; sudden death."

The hairs on the back of my neck started to prickle. I'd had no idea that Pelkanitracin was so dangerous. None of the brochures I'd read mentioned these sorts of side effects. The rep was such a nice young lady, and she'd said the drug was one of the best. Who can you believe these days? I read the warnings one more time to make sure I wasn't mistaken, trying to remember if I'd prescribed Pelkanitracin for anyone else. I thought not.

"The bad news is that you have at least 22 multiple personalities. The good news is that qualifies you for our group rate."

"Well, Mr. Kerslake, I strongly recommend that you give up marathon running."

My confidence was quite shaken as I went into the next exam room. Fortunately the patient was in only to have sutures removed — not much room for error there. Mr. Zotemia had been in a week ago to have a cyst removed from his back. I'd thought it was a simple sebaceous cyst, but it had turned out to be a fibrous tumour that had taken more effort to remove than I'd anticipated. I'd had to insert a dozen sutures to close the incision, and I remembered joking with Mr. Zotemia that the scar would compete with the nephrectomy scar he sported on the other side of his back.

It took only a few minutes to take the sutures out of the incision on Alan Zotemia's back. The wound was well healed. I opened the chart to make a note of what I'd done and spotted the pathology report on the specimen I'd sent off last week.

"Ah — " I started, but my throat seemed to close up as I read the pathologist's report: "The specimen appears to be renal tissue."

What!

"The organ does not appear to be intact, but a large portion of a kidney is identified."

I gulped and looked up at Alan. He did look a little pale.

"How're you feeling?" I asked, trying to sound casual. "Peeing okay?"

*"I'm sorry, but I don't work on a
'you-show-me-yours-and-I'll-show-you-mine' basis."*

"Well, now that you mention it, Doc, I have been a bit tired. What's wrong?"

"It looks as though . . . um. It seems that, er . . ." I was finding it difficult to word what I was trying to say. "It appears that we, I mean I, removed your kidney. It wasn't a cyst, after all."

"Well, it was a much easier operation than the last time," Alan said, grinning.

"I don't think you understand. It's sort of serious not to have any kidneys. You'll have to see a specialist, very soon."

"Okay, Doc. I'll think about that when I come back from my vacation."

"No, really, you can't wait." I could hear my voice rising in desperation as he started to walk out of the room.

"Don't worry, Doc. I can handle it." He grinned again, and as he left the office, and I was left standing, my mind racked with a mixture of disbelief, guilt, and fear.

It seemed, though, that I was the only one so stricken. My nurse, smiling politely, guided me to the next patient. "Remind me to call him later," I said, pointing in the direction of the now-departed Alan Zotemia.

"Of course," she replied, and I felt like a child being comforted.

"It's serious. He's got a bad problem." Again she smiled politely. Didn't anybody understand? "Melena has an earache," she said, nodding toward the next exam room.

"Melena Snigglypoof?" My nurse nodded with what I considered a malicious smile. I thought the day had already become as bad as it could get.

Mrs. Snigglypoof was sitting on a chair in the exam room with her daughter on her knee. The four-year-old girl was a miniature — if that's the right word — replica of her mother: blonde, round of face and body, and with a disposition that demonstrated an antagonism to the rest of the human race.

"So you have an earache, do you, Melena?" I started with a subtle approach.

"She certainly has. Again," said her mother with a look that suggested I was clearly to blame for her daughter's malady.

"Well, let's have a look at it," I said, moving toward the duo. Melena immediately put both hands up to her head and covered her ears.

"There, there, he's not going to hurt you," crooned her mother, glaring at me as if I'd just struck her child.

"No, just a little look. It won't take long."

The girl shook her head violently as I approached, and her mother hugged her away from me. "Let me read to her for a while," Mrs. Snigglypoof said. "That usually calms her down." She picked up a book she'd been carrying and opened it. It was *Caribbean* by James Michener. "She loves it when it gets to the bit about Francis Drake," the mother added, and began reading.

When it became obvious that Francis Drake wouldn't be making his appearance for at least a week, I interrupted. "If I could examine her ear, then you could take her home and read to her there."

Mrs. Snigglypoof ignored me. Well, almost ignored me. She gave a little shake of her head and said, "Shush."

I could hear impatient sounds of waiting patients from the other side of the exam room door. "Please, Mrs. Snigglypoof, I haven't got all day." I moved closer and got out my otoscope.

Melena screamed and her mother kept on reading. I grabbed the hand that covered the ear in question and prised it from her head. The girl immediately replaced it and turned away. I managed to remove it again and grabbed at her ear. Mrs. Snigglypoof continued to read in a monotone. Melena was shaking her head now, determined that I wasn't going to look in her ear. I gripped the ear firmly and got the otoscope to it. She shook her head again and I gripped harder. Just a couple of seconds, I thought. That's all I need to get a look. She struggled some more, and I pulled at her ear. I was almost there.

And then, with a startling suddenness, I felt something give. There was a tearing sound and a squeal from Melena. I looked at my hand and there, held between my thumb and index finger, was Melena's ear. For an insane instant I had the urge to slap it back on her head to see if it would stick.

"Look what you've done!" Mrs. Snigglypoof said, staring at the ear.

I could feel her and her daughter's accusing eyes on me. I looked down at the ear in my hand and then at the two glaring females. "Do you believe in the ear fairy?" was all I could think to ask.

I left the room in a daze. What was happening today? Everything was going wrong.

"Baby Oopsorry is here for his circumcision," my nurse said. "I have the tray ready." I looked at my shaking hands and decided I wasn't quite ready to wield sharp steel anywhere near Baby Oopsorry's genitals. Sitting in my office, I closed my eyes, and tried to slow my racing pulse.

The telephone brought me to my senses. I opened my eyes and felt disoriented. I was in my bedroom, and it was my bedside phone that was ringing. On the floor was a copy of *Malpractice Monthly*, open at an article entitled "Malpractice Is Not for the Malpractitioner Only — A Look at How You Could Be the Next Victim."

So it was a dream, or a nightmare. Serves me right for reading scary articles before going to sleep at night. I picked up the phone. "Hello," said the voice on the line. "This is Percival Hans from the legal firm of Hans, Neese, and Bompsedayse. I represent the Mumblechuck family. I wonder if we could meet?"

— DR. JOHN EGERTON

"They're all jealous, of course, because I conquered my paranoia."

Overheard

Two men discussing a friend's ailment: "I heard Joe's laid up in bed with back pain. The doctor told him it's his psychotic nerve."

"Yeah, I heard the pain gets so bad it can drive you crazy."

Female patient to GP: "Can you refer me to a groinacologist?"

Man on hearing doctor's diagnosis of his child's condition: "I don't understand how he could have chicken pox. We had him annihilated when he was younger."

Woman to doctor: "I've been feeling absolutely marvellous since starting those frolic acid tablets."

Woman relating her sister's experience in hospital: "The doctors had to seduce her labour as she was carrying 11 pounds of fluid!"

Man consulting doctor on how to deal with alcoholic wife: "We got her into hospital, but she admitted herself out."

All in the Family

Several years ago I was taking the initial history from a rural Saskatchewan Farmer of Eastern European origin. This middle-aged man had a long-standing history of asthma and rhinitis and multiple inhalant allergies.

I'd just finished taking an exhaustive family history, which revealed a very strong familial tendency for similar complaints, when the patient offered his own opinion.

"You know, Doc," he said, "they say these here allergies are inherited, but heck, I know a lot of people who got 'em that ain't related to me!"

— DR. D. W. COCKCROFT

Listen to the Patient — A Lesson in the Art of Medicine

One of the first lessons drilled into us at medical school was: "Listen to the patient." It was alleged that if we'd only learn to listen, all would be revealed. When I look back on that bit of wisdom now, it seems to me to be "kind of" true. I also agree with the adage that if you haven't got the diagnosis by the end of the history, you probably won't have it by the end of the examination.

The problem is that patients have been known, on occasion, to drone on a little. Like about 30 minutes maybe, with only a few gems of relevant information to keep the doctor's mind alive. The following true story will demonstrate the value of listening to the patient.

The patient in question was, shall we say, difficult. Every practice has one: demanding, cranky, multisymptomatic ("It's me knee, me bum, me elbow"), dissatisfied ("Dr. Jones used to know what to do"), doubting ("I think it should be taken out"), and threatening ("Don't blame me if it gets worse in the night").

This one was a classic — angry at the hand that fate had dealt her, with a rotten husband and miserable kids. Her outlet was the manipulation of the medical profession. Our notes on her were three inches thick. She knew every specialist for miles around and had reasons why she didn't want to see *that* one again.

She queried every suggested treatment, knew every drug, and claimed allergy to about ten of them. She could give you three reasons why the one you suggested was no use; meanwhile, the one she wanted was usually habit-forming.

When her name appeared on the morning list, depression set in early and burnout struck by noon. (To be quite fair, though, she did help pay off the mortgage.)

During one memorable episode of abdominal pain, she was bound and determined to have her gall bladder out. Eventually, as you might expect, after numerous referrals, she found

"The big problem with your illness, Mr. Hawkins, is that nobody famous has caught it yet."

someone several towns away who relieved her of the gall bladder (but not the pain). She looked uncharacteristically satisfied when she returned to show us her fresh scar and told us, "The surgeon said it was full of sludge, which could have turned into a stone." There was no insight into the fact that the pain hadn't changed.

We had several partners in our practice at that time, and we all knew this patient. On the particular weekend that relates to this story, the most volatile and least sympathetic of the partners was on call.

At 11:30 p.m. the patient demanded a house call. Terrible stomach pain, couldn't get to the hospital, husband was away. Nowadays we'd send an ambulance, but back then the patient would be visited first.

She lived way out in the countryside, down a narrow, dark road that boasted a series of small, messy, half-finished houses surrounded by old cars and farm equipment. It was an area well-known to the police, who were often out on Saturday nights, stopping domestic fights and locating stolen property.

So off the partner went into the darkness, finally managing to find the small road, then the unlit, unmarked house. He parked in the muddy driveway, and struggled to the side door.

On examining the patient, he discovered there was nothing wrong with her at all. She was drunk and maudlin, lonely and mad at her husband, who'd left her again.

The partner blew his top. Dragged out of home on a cold night, taking hours to find the damn place, getting mud in his shoes from the driveway, and then finding that the call was completely unnecessary! She was a useless drunk, a disgrace, a pain in the neck (or lower)! There was never a damn thing wrong with her; it was the last time he'd ever be dragged out to see her!

He ranted and raved, and raved and ranted, while putting away his equipment, closing his bag, and making for the front door. She tried to interrupt several times, but once he was in full swing he was not to be stopped. His furious denunciation reached a climax as he flung open the door, stepped out with an angry flourish — and fell four feet down to the path.

She'd been trying to tell him there were no front steps.

So they were right all along back in medical school when they told us: listen to the patient.

— DR. JOHN COCKER

"You're a hypochondriac.
Take two placebos and call me in the morning."

A Poor Fit

Things aren't always what they seem, as I was to discover one day during a routine afternoon. A young girl entered my office with an older woman who appeared to be her mother. The girl was approximately 14 years old, and the older person turned out to be her sister.The girl looked slightly embarrassed when I asked her what the problem was.

"I need an operation," she murmured.

"What sort of operation?" I asked.

"You know, down there. My boyfriend says I'm too loose and I need an operation to make it tighter."

Somewhat shocked at such a statement coming from an apparently innocent young girl (I was fairly new at medical practice then), I proceeded to examine her "down there." Everything seemed to be in order, and I reassured her that she was perfectly normal and didn't need an operation to "tighten things up."

She appeared unconvinced by my reassurance and insisted that this was a serious matter and she was afraid to lose her boyfriend. By this time I was getting a bit annoyed with this boyfriend's attitude, so I told her that perhaps he was "too small."

Upon hearing this, her sister, who'd remained quiet until now, jumped up and said, "That's what I told her." With that they both left, the patient still looking unconvinced, but the older sister seemingly satisfied that she'd been right all along.

I guess you can't please all of the people all of the time.

— DR. T. A. ROHLAND

Communication Breakdown

When I was a student, I sat in on a vascular surgeon's out-patient clinic. Before each patient came in the surgeon quickly reviewed the case notes and gave me the gist of the problem.

He spent a little extra time on one particular set of notes and said to me, "I'm really worried about this man. He has very severe thromboangiitis obliterans and he's gradually losing bits of fingers and toes. He's also had a couple of moderately severe coronary occlusions.

"One of the problems is that he's an extremely heavy smoker and he won't give up. He knows it's going to kill him, but he simply will not stop. He was here a month ago, and I really read the riot act to him.

"I told him that every cigarette was a nail in his coffin and that if he didn't throw his cigarettes away, he'd be dead in a year or two. 'Alcohol isn't a problem,' I said to him. 'Any amount of alcohol won't harm your arteries, but you've got to stop smoking or else!' That was a month ago. Let's see how he's doing now."

"You're not my normal doctor."

The nurse ushered an ill-looking man into the consulting room. He stumbled as he made his way to a chair, he slumped as he sat, and he looked as though he might slide sideways onto the floor. His eyes were glassy and his tongue seemed thick when he spoke.

"How are you feeling today, Mr. MacDonald?" the surgeon asked.

"G'eat, Doctor, g'eat! Ev'r sinsh you put me on that drink treatment, I've been perfect!"

— DR. ALISTAIR MUNRO

Computer Balk

Yesterday was cold, rainy, and depressing. The only thing good about yesterday was that it wasn't Monday. A summer day should be sunny and warm, not the kind of day we had yesterday, requiring raincoats, hats, boots, and that extra bit of sanity that just can't be recalled. What to do?

Off to the *mall!*

Summertime at the mall evokes feelings that are positively primordial. Seeing old friends, getting out of the rain, downing a salt-cholesterol-sugar treat in the "bistro quarter," watching one another trying to look our best (some of us succeeding better than others), and visiting the technology store for a look at the computer stuff.

Boyd, the manager, always remembers me, salutes me by name, recalls what I do, and asks me about it. Friendly fellow, good at his job, but doesn't know a thing about computers, except to tell me that since graduation this spring most of his have been sold. My knowledge of computers is on a par with his: I bought his last one.

He does have a bright young chap right out of computer school who can tell me over the phone how to reinsert, from the supplemental program discs, a factory-installed program that the kids erased one day when they should have been hanging around some video arcade or strip mall. He's quick and efficient.

But his tongue flaps with that strange syntax known to newscasters and anthropologists as computerese (rhymes with ease, disease, trapeze, and sleaze). Perfectly good English words now prompt a mild startle reflex in my autonomic adrenaline-producing system, and I have a strong desire toward flight.

Another fine young comput-o-chap came to our office to install our new computer, and he spoke the same tongue. My adrenaline defence mechanisms have hardened since Boyd sold us a 640K with no hard drive (for the children), so I laughed off the invariable bad news concerning why the brand-new office machine wouldn't go.

"Junk," the young computer fellow said. "The board is gone. We'll have one of our repairmen come round early next week. Pure junk!"

"Oh, whatever do you mean?" asked Jane, the secretary of our office, who had earlier agreed to be in charge of said computer. I myself prefer not to touch one if possible. After all, she has a brother who has a couple of degrees in computers and she worked the one we borrowed to complete an article last summer. She worked it well, so I (myself) don't need to. She had a direct and intense interest in what the young comput-o-chap was getting at, although I think she had a fair idea just the same.

"Just what I said. Junk. It's always happening. These things are junk!"

Our computer had followed this path to reach us: *Ten months* — approved by Central Administration. *Eight months* — ordered after much debate regarding compatibility with

Central's mainframes (there are three we must compatibilize with). *Four months* — received at Computer Services and detained there for questioning. *Two weeks* — delivered to Jane's crowded desk.

"Junk," the young computer fellow repeated. "These machines are junk. The boards are always going. Every time you turn it on it automatically boots itself up."

If the machine were animate, I'd feel a certain pity for it, seeing as how he put it that way. Although booting it up is what I'd most like to do to every computer I come in contact with.

But not Jane. "Won't that be expensive?" She seemed worried that she'd have to go about pulling administrative teeth to get the resources for the repairs and for the now required but previously unauthorized new desk. The computer currently sits on her old desk in the middle of the only way into the office.

We'd been waiting ten months. We could wait that long and longer. We're tough. Perhaps the young computer fellow caught a sense of where she was coming from, for he spoke quickly with equal portions of authority and assurance.

"No probleem-oh! The guy will be here first thing early in the week."

When the machine finally gets going, my research capacity will be increased. Dread and despair! One of our mainframes connects to my buddies over in research. We've done some projects together, and now I'm fearful they'll be E-mailing data and expecting me to use things with names like D-Base, SPSS-X, NSP-PC, and other weirdness. Sometimes when my research buddies get talking that computerese my palms and soles sweat, my heart races, my head spins, and I feel like lying down.

Computers are complex, as are our reactions to them. Quiet, intelligent, and otherwise sensible-appearing people crop up at intimate dinner parties regaling all comers with tales of programs, discs, modems, and monitors. Puts one off one's dinner. Mine, anyway.

When I tell them, or others of their ilk, about our home computer (the one with 640K and no hard drive), they all talk computerese.

"Junk!" the less polite say.

"Have you seen the Whiz-wuz at Hardware Land? It's got two hard drives. It would be so much faster than . . ." the better bred pontificate.

"Oh, did you?" the faint-of-heart ask with embarrassment, then change the topic to their latest software package that saved them $22,000 in taxes last year or holds every recipe printed in the English language.

They all mean "junk."

"Without a hard drive you can't do anything," an acquaintance exhaled once, almost in tears (where he's coming from I wouldn't want to know).

One lady told me she and her husband had four computers and he had two at the office. They spend 16 hours a day sitting at their keyboards saving time.

One of the guys at work can tell us in three seconds whether or not he's booked at 3:00 p.m. on the first Tuesday of August for the next 68 years. He spends so much time setting up his life that it has passed him by. But he's much faster now than when he was byte-less.

An older, seemingly experienced person that I know got his university-aged children a computer, and now it's all he talks about. He writes reams of stuff. We get memos on all kinds of uselessness that look really nice because he bought two expensive word processing programs and his third really expensive computer.

If encouraged, these kindhearted but misdirected souls offer to copy their favourite programs or come over and show you (me, really) how to get the most out of your (my) stuff. Boyd never offers these things; he doesn't know how. But he did offer me a deal on a laptop.

You see, I have a confession to make. I use our home computer. But only for the word processor. My kids, of course, can make the thing work. They can get any program to run. They play games for hours, especially when the sun shines.

When it rains, they seem strangely satiated with the box and we have to go off to the mall. Off to see Boyd who, despite being surrounded by the things, knows nothing about them. He doesn't talk computerese, just services and money. Our money.

Oh, well, he tells me in the fall the hard drives will go on sale. So for the kids we'll have to buy one. Not that it will make my life better. I only use the writing part of these machines so I can interface, link up, and connect meaningfully with you, dear readers. Thank you. As always I remain . . .

— DR. BILL EATON

Feet First

A middle-aged epileptic frequented my office about once a month. His problem was complicated with alcohol and multiple fractures sustained during seizures while under the influence.

It was his routine when he came to my office that unless I was actually waiting for him in the examining room, he would take off his shoe and sock to show me his bunion. He had probably the worst-smelling foot that one could ever be unfortunate enough to encounter.

It was therefore my practice to make certain that I was in the examining room when he arrived and not allow him to take his shoe off.

It was on one of these occasions that he complained of some visual problems, and I referred him to the local eye specialist for examination. About a month later I received a call from the optometrist, who said that he had this gentleman

*"In the first place, yes, I did warn your
client about using the suppository after drinking.
In the second place, I'm amazed he could
insert it after 15 bottles of beer."*

in his office with his shoe off and wondered why he was there to see him.

"He wanted his eyes checked," I said, chuckling to myself as I thought that he certainly had a novel way of getting prompt attention.

I'm now waiting to hear from the local dentist.

— DR. G. B. GRIGGS

What's on, Doc?

If we've learned anything from the Meech Lake melee and the Charlottetown Accord referendum, it's just how fragile the Canadian confederation really is. We know now that all it takes is some political pouting, posturing, and paranoia by the premiers and, poof, we have to worry about whistling "Yankee Doodle."

Some pro-Americans have always argued that without the unique French flavour provided by Quebec, Canadians are just

"You're perfectly healthy — at least two days to live."

Americans, anyway. After all, what truly unique cultural characteristics make us (dare I say) a distinct society? Strangely shaped bacon and five percent beer? That's hardly enough to base a country on. Hockey? Hey, Wayne Gretzky lives in L.A. now. And English Canadians certainly don't have a unique language . . . unless you count the "eh?" we could put into U.S.A.

Even if we've never wanted to be Americans, all of us have had to wonder lately what it would be like to join the United States. That may be the reason behind the startling news I've just uncovered — CBC-TV is planning to capitalize on this new interest in things American. Forget Tommy Hunter and *Front Page Challenge* — my information suggests that the CBC is gearing up for a full-scale plunge into American-style TV programming.

And what type of shows do Americans like? Apparently the CBC's researchers have narrowed it down to two perennial themes: cops and doctors. Since we Canadians are a notoriously law-abiding lot, cop shows are out, so the CBC has opted to gamble its scarce funds on the wholesale production of prime time TV series about doctors.

Of course, medicine will be different in the nineties, so the CBC series will have to have some new wrinkles on the tried-and-true doctor theme. Here's a sampling:

- **C*A*S*H**. A show about the zany antics of a madcap financial department at a hospital owned by a major health-care conglomerate. Led by Hawkeye, a talented cost accountant (his nickname comes from an uncanny ability to spot a slashable expense from a mile away), the series also features Radar, a bill collector with a sixth sense about where deadbeat ex-patients are hiding. Week after week the cast finds a world of wacky ways to make sure their hospital's bottom line is tops.
- **Prince Edward Island Son**. All about a native doctor from Summerside who's torn between the ways of the modern world and the traditions of his ancestors (from the days before Brian Mulroney came to power).
- **St. Send-Them-Elsewhere**. A prime time soap that takes place in a super-ritzy private hospital that's so exclusive even emergency patients need an engraved invitation to

be admitted. The show focuses on the lives and loves of the dedicated men and women who must deal every day with the stress of administering liposuction and tummy tucks to the filthy rich.
- **Trapper Jean, M.D.** (that's Jean as in Chrétien). The adventures of a doctor in Canada's Far North. Unable to get by on what the government pays him for his services, and cut off from his northern allowance, he's forced to moonlight as a fur trapper in order to survive. In the series pilot the fur really flies when Dr. Jean saves the life of a rich tourist, only to have her refuse to pay the bill because she turns out to be a dedicated animal rights activist.
- **Marcus Wellbeing, M.D.** A sitcom for the nineties, about a West Coast doctor who uses the latest New Age techniques to treat his patients, including herbalism, astrology, alchemy, aura therapy, and crystal power. For especially tough cases Marcus performs channelling and lets his body be taken over by Moo-La, a 10,000-year-old healer being from the ninth dimension.

Our sources say the CBC is hoping this kind of sensational U.S.- style television will be a smash, thanks to the constitutional brouhaha.

Oh, say, can you see . . . are there any *Beachcomber* reruns on?

— DANNY DOWHAL

Unexplained Weight Loss?

One of my more embarrassing moments in practice occurred about 15 years ago. At the time I was one of two physicians in a small community in northern Cape Breton. Maternity patients would see both of us for checkups during the course of pregnancy. Whoever was on call when a woman presented in labour would look after the delivery. We kept each other informed but occasionally there were lapses.

One evening a somewhat hefty young woman came to my office for a prenatal visit, or so I thought. I'd seen her a number of times during her pregnancy but not in the previous few

*"What do you mean, plain old stress?
It must be executive stress, surely."*

weeks. I noted on her chart that it was just about her due date. I asked how she was feeling and checked her blood pressure, urine, and weight.

Checking her chart, I noted a 20-pound weight loss since her last visit 10 days earlier. Thinking I'd made a mistake, I asked her to get on the scale again. There was still a 20-pound discrepancy.

"According to the scale, you've lost 20 pounds," I commented.

"Yes . . . I had the baby last week."

— DR. KENNETH MURRAY

Proverbs

Every invalid is a physician. (Irish)

Medicine can only cure curable diseases, and then not always. (Chinese)

Sickness comes on horseback and departs on foot. (Dutch)

An imaginary ailment is worse than a disease. (Yiddish)

Show him death and he'll be content with fever. (Persian)

Sleep to the sick is half health. (German)

People who take cold baths never have rheumatism, but they have cold baths. (American)

An ailing woman lives forever. (Spanish)

The best surgeon is he that hath been hacked himself. (English)

Only a fool will make a doctor his heir. (Russian)

"OO, OO, OO, OO, OO, OO, OO..."

The Creative Use of Disease
How to Put Your Ailments
to Work for You

When I started practice, I assumed that patients came in to have their diseases or symptoms cured. It took me a long time to realize that for some people an illness is a weapon to use against the world or to control their environment.

They may have taught this at medical school, but I don't remember it. Possibly I was dozing at the time and missed it. Or perhaps it's just so obvious to everyone else that they didn't bother to mention it. Anyhow, in those early days I'd spend a lot of time investigating and treating symptoms that the patient had no intention of relinquishing.

"Not tonight, dear. I have a headache" is a classic use of a symptom to modify the behaviour patterns of another person. Similarly, "You'll have to be quiet. Mommy has a headache" has surely been used throughout human history to keep children in line.

Having a small symptom or a minor, nonfatal disease can help any of us survive in a hostile world. How about a knee that hurts if you have to stand by the sink to do the dishes, or an ankle that doesn't hurt enough to stop you doing what you want to do, but causes sufficient pain to prevent you from doing undesirable things?

Any list of convenient ailments that can be disabling, yet defy lavish laboratory tests, would include arthritis, back pain, chronic fatigue syndrome, headache, and allergies. Is it mere coincidence that such conditions are the ones most frequently treated by practitioners of "alternative medicine"?

It's not entirely strange that alternative medicine doesn't seek to treat acute appendicitis, fractured femur, or acute myocardial infarction. Patients know well enough that if they have a real disease, they need to seek real medical help.

Let me suggest one condition that you might like to consider for your own personal arsenal of weapons to use against the world. I'd always considered hypoglycemia to be a nondisease in that it causes an array of nonspecific symptoms that don't correlate to any known lab test. However, my views began to change when I heard of a surgeon who had five children, but only one wife. This meant that her time was at a premium. The surgeon developed hypoglycemia; the attacks were so severe that his wife had to drop whatever she was doing and prepare him some food.

This treatment was so successful that he hadn't actually had an attack for many years. It made me appreciate once again the importance of preventative measures, and also made me think that hypoglycemia wasn't so bad, after all. Who knows? Maybe a little dose of it might be in order for myself.

In fact, I have to stop writing now because I feel an attack coming on. I must get my wife to stop what she's doing and cook something for me right away.

Excuse me . . .

— DR. JOHN COCKER

One of Those Moments

I am a general surgeon and do a considerable amount of plastic surgery. I live in a rural community where there are numerous thin, shapely cowgirls present, many of whom I've done mammoplasty on.

On one occasion a young cowgirl appeared in the office for some minor complaints, and I asked, "Oh, incidentally, how are your breasts?"

She looked rather surprised and said, "They're fine."

"Have you had any hardening forming at all?" I asked.

"No, not a bit."

"Well, let's check them," I said. "Yes, they seem quite nice and soft and they look good, too."

"Yes, I think so, too." she said.

I failed to look for any scar, but there usually isn't much, anyway. After she left the office, I began to wonder about the case and asked my nurse if I'd done a mammoplasty on her. Much to my surprise and chagrin, she said I hadn't!

So this proved to be one of my most embarrassing moments and, of course, I had to phone her and apologize.

"Well, that's okay," she said, "but I did wonder why you were so interested in my breasts."

— DR. B. J. LARSON

"I can't see you as my partner, but I'd like you to know
you're everything I look for in a patient."

Divine Inspiration

Having a large asthma practice, I spend a great deal of time attempting to convince asthmatic patients of the need for compliance with inhaled prophylactic medications.

I was having a particularly frustrating time with an otherwise intelligent Irish Catholic priest. His corticosteroid-dependent asthma required regular ingested corticosteroid for control and yet his compliance with inhaled corticosteroids was dismal.

I came up with an idea which, at the time, was relatively new. I suggested that the inhaled corticosteroid should be used regularly prior to meals. In that way it could be left in a conspicuous place on the table, perhaps beside the salt and pepper. Furthermore, eating a meal after the medication had been inhaled should be a valuable way to rinse out the mouth and thus help to prevent topical candida infection.

When I explained this approach to the good father, he thought for a while and then, with a gleam in his eye, said, "Yes, I know just what I'll do.

"I'll hold the inhaler like this." He grasped it in a pious gesture between his hands. "Then I'll go like this." He bowed his head even more piously. "And then I'll say, 'Let us spray!'"

— DR. D. W. COCKCROFT

All Teed Off

Timely Tales of Fairways and Foul

The story goes that a keen Canadian golfer was invited by a good friend in England to play on a prestigious golf course during his forthcoming visit to Britain. Shortly after arriving, he was informed by his friend that he couldn't make it to the club himself, but had made arrangements for the Canadian to play with the club professional.

This course is notable in that the two nines are separated by a motorway (expressway). The ninth hole runs alongside the motorway, which is obscured by a large hedge. The Canadian visitor stood at the ninth tee and produced an enormous slice, which carried the ball through the hedge and out toward the motorway. The club pro immediately moved off in the direction of the ball, saying that he knew exactly where he was likely to find it.

Half an hour elapsed before he returned to the ninth tee, looking ashen-faced. "You won't believe this," he said. "Your ball hit a motorcyclist on the motorway and he crashed. A large truck overturned trying to avoid the motorcyclist. The truck caught fire. Five other vehicles piled into the back of the truck. It appears that at least seven people are dead — it's absolute carnage out there!"

"My God!" the appalled Canadian said. "What am I going to do?"

"Well," the pro said, "perhaps if you relaxed your grip and closed your stance a little . . . "

I was reminded of this story recently when I hooked my ball onto a long stretch of water along the right-hand side of the tenth fairway at Greystone Golf Club in Milton, Ontario. I'd been invited with three friends to try out what has been described as one of the finest new courses in North America.

Certainly the setting is spectacular, and the tees, fairways, and greens are of Pencross bent grass, which makes you feel that you're walking on a lush green carpet. Personally I was inhibited, as it seemed sacrilegious to take a divot of such beautiful grass, and so I had more than my usual share of topped shots.

If I had my problems on the tenth hole, however, one of my fellow sleuths by the name of Watson had his troubles elsewhere. He spent an inordinate amount of time getting through, rather than over, a deep ravine in front of the eighth green.

Watson is a Scotsman, fluent in Gaelic, and was moved by his experience to characterize each hole in Gaelic, in a manner that was established long ago at the Old Course at St. Andrew's, Scotland. Thus the eighth hole was named *Sloc mor*, which means a big pit.

Watson isn't noted for his bunker play, and when we arrived at the 17th tee and saw a cluster of bunkers in the corner of the dog-leg left, he cried, "This hole is named *A'Ghriuthlach*," likening the bunkers to a rash of measles.

At the end of the round the consensus was that we'd all like to play the course again, because inevitably we'd missed many of the subtleties of architectural design the first time around. But we didn't push our luck, unlike the ardent golfer who arrived home late one evening after promising his wife he'd be home at lunchtime.

"Well, darling," he said, "I was just driving out of the club when I saw a gorgeous blonde standing by a red sports car that had a flat tire. She looked quite helpless, so I stopped and helped her change the tire.

"She was so grateful that she invited me for a drink at a nearby bar. We had a few drinks there and we got on so well

CHRIS
KEMP

"It's definitely an ear infection. I recommend you lay off the phone sex for a while."

that she asked me back to her house for cocktails. I didn't want to appear ungracious, and what's more she was one of the most beautiful women I've ever seen.

"After a few more drinks at her place, we got very friendly indeed, and I'm afraid to tell you, darling, that we did actually go to bed together."

"You lying bastard!" his wife cried. "You played 36 holes today!"

— DR. JOHN GATELY

Nature's Way

One evening I was sitting in my office just tidying up a few things when a shy rap came at the back door of the clinic. The caller proved to be a plump young lady in her early twenties, who indicated rather hesitantly that she had a serious problem.

I ushered her into my office and inquired as to the nature of her difficulty. She dropped her slacks and pointed at a length of pink rubber tubing descending from the anus, like a rudimentary tail.

It seems she'd been trying to administer an enema to herself when the enema tubing became firmly lodged and wouldn't move. I attempted some gentle traction, while firmly biting my lip to avoid any appearance of levity. No result.

I tried pushing the tube in further and then withdrawing. Still no result. Finally I twisted, turned, and otherwise manipulated the tube in every possible way, with similar lack of success.

I decided I'd better give the local surgeon a call and see if he had any suggestions. I left the patient on the table in the left lateral decubitus position while I picked up the phone, dialled the number, and took a sip of coffee from the mug I'd been sipping from before the arrival of my unexpected caller.

As I described the situation to the surgeon and detailed my lack of success, there was a sudden explosive flatus from the patient and the tube flew out, landing business end first in my coffee cup and splattering me and my desk in the process.

"Never mind," I said to the consultant. "The situation seems to have rectified itself."

— DR. GEORGE BURDEN

Holy Terror

Medical Science vs. Established Religion

When I first went to Nova Scotia, I bought a medical practice from a young man called Bill Maddock. He'd started just after internship, meaning to stay a while, but after only two years, exhaustion had set in, so he decided to return to his studies.

It was an extremely busy practice, and often I didn't get to bed or change my clothes for as long as seven days and nights in a row. Sometimes the smell was enough to attract comment!

When I was in one of these phases, I'd try to snatch a few minutes' sleep here and there on the lazyboy chair in the living room, or sometimes at night on the way back from house calls I'd pull into a logging track and fall asleep in the car. I once woke up in the car, looked at my watch, and saw that it was eight o'clock, but didn't know if it was eight in the morning or eight at night. I had to wait until the light changed — it was morning!

As I say, this Bill was an earnest young fellow, and I remember him saying to me, "Alan, I don't think I should give

"Now listen to me. I want you to go out there and say, 'Today I'm going to fly.'"

you any advice, and I really don't mean to, but there is one thing I want to mention. Virtually all of the patients here are Roman Catholic and, as you can guess, the priest is very powerful in the community. I know the church is against birth control, so I decided not to have anything to do with it. Of course, what you do is up to you, but I just thought I should at least tell you about it."

It was nice of him, and I certainly thought about it, but eventually I dealt with the problem quite differently. It seemed to me that birth control was a matter for the individual to decide, and if it was all right with his or (more usually) her conscience, then I should help in every way. However, from then on I could never forget Bill's warning about the priest, who might not be too happy about the way I was treating his flock, to say the least.

Mind you, some of my patients had a lot of children. One of them had 17, another 19, and one had 21. So the idea of birth control, in some cases at least, didn't seem to me to be too unreasonable.

"That's the beauty of a placebo.
It just gives the illusion of an overdose."

My approach was to bring up the subject of birth control in a noncommittal way and then let the patient make up her own mind. If she showed interest, I arranged it and supplied her with pills or some other appropriate method.

It didn't take long for the news to get around, and soon birth control was a popular "item" in my practice. All the time, though, I had the thought at the back of my mind that the priest was out there somewhere, and it wouldn't be long before I heard from him in no uncertain terms.

I had a nurse called Elizabeth, who was a mixture of Irish and French. The patients used to wait in the waiting room, which was built on the back of my house. To get to me, they'd have to pass through a little room where I kept all the pills. That was where, of course, all the birth-control materials were kept.

Elizabeth would always announce the patients formally in a grand voice with her own distinctive accent.

"Monsieur and Madame Remy Leblanc!"

She would then usher them into my office. It was a simple place with the usual furniture — a desk and chair, a couch, a cabinet full of frightening instruments, and two kitchen chairs on which sat the patient and the relative.

One day Elizabeth came running into my office in an absolute panic. "Dr. Lupin, Dr. Lupin, Father's here!"

"Well, Elizabeth, show him in," I said with a sinking feeling.

"But, Dr. Lupin, it's Father, you understand? It's Father!"

"I know, Elizabeth. Well, show him in!"

"But, Dr. Lupin, it's *Father.* It's *Father. Father's* here!"

"For God's sake, Elizabeth. Take hold of yourself and show him in!"

She went out. There was a short pause. I waited while Father's heavy footsteps passed through the little room where all the evil materials were kept. Elizabeth came to the door and announced in a shaky voice, "F-father Grouard." And through the door came the priest.

He was a large, heavily built man, with beetling eyebrows and full red cheeks. He wore a long black cassock and stood in the doorway looking at me very seriously and for what seemed to be a very long time. This is it, I thought.

He spoke. "Dr. Lupin."

"Yes, Father," I answered.

"Dr. Lupin . . ."

"How do you do, Father?"

"Dr. Lupin . . ."

These were the first words he'd ever spoken to me. I knew something was coming. There was a long pause.

"Dr. Lupin, there's nothing wrong with kissing a nun."

I stared at him blankly. I didn't know what to think.

He glowered at me and continued. "But you mustn't get into the habit! *Haargh, haargh, haargh!*"

And he slapped his knee, and laughed and laughed until the tears ran down his face.

— DR. ALAN LUPIN

The Last Resort

Pediatricians need, early in their professional careers, to become accustomed to dealing with reluctant and recalcitrant patients. Tenants of adjacent medical offices have been known to

complain about the howls emanating from pediatricians'
examining rooms. The staff in a pediatric office must become
adept at dealing with the "reluctant drag-ins." And at the end of
the day the pediatrician has to have developed a philosophy of
forbearance, or at least resignation, in order to survive.

I was fortunate that I had enough years behind me that this
philosophy was at least partially developed when Tony was
brought in for a checkup.

Tony was four years old. He'd been coming for well-baby
examinations during his first year of life and semiannual examinations during his second and third years, with no intimation
of what was to occur when he was four.

Sometime during the previous year he and his parents had
moved from Sault Sainte Marie to Toronto. At about the time of
his fourth birthday Tony was visiting his grandparents in Sault
Sainte Marie, and his grandmother and aunt had been
instructed to bring him in for his four-year checkup. As it
turned out, Tony had other ideas.

An indication of what was to come was audible as Tony and
his escort approached my waiting room. My staff and other
patients were alarmed by the shrieks. Tony was dragged
through the waiting room, past the staff desk, and finally, with
loud wails of protest, moved into an examining room and the
door was shut. I waited a few minutes before entering, in the

"You're right, Doc, it is a miracle cure. I'll have another."

hope that Tony would run out of breath and his grandma and aunt would get him calmed down.

At last, armed with stethoscope, flashlight, tongue depressor, and aurascope, and robed in my uniform of white lab coat, I made my entry, to be greeted by a distinct amplification of the basal pandemonium.

My initial instinct was to retreat. However, inveterate professionalism would not permit this course of action. Furthermore, there was my pride to consider, and also the fact that this little boy had been transported 500 miles specifically to be examined by me. I could hardly let him down.

I advanced courageously toward the examining table, stethoscope earpieces in place, stethoscope bell in hand, and aurascope at the ready. Tony's grandmother and aunt were struggling valiantly to fulfill their role in the proceedings. They were getting buffeted about, but they managed to get one of Tony's arms out of his shirt and one shoe off. His grandma's glasses were askew and his aunt's necklace had rattled onto the floor.

Tony meanwhile was screaming imprecations, struggling mightily and effectively, but when he finally understood that his own strength might not prevail, he commenced a beseechment for aid. First it was to his mother, then his father,

"Medical science isn't that simple, Mrs. Tremblay.
You can't just shop around until you find a disease you like."

but they were 500 miles away and he seemed to realize fairly quickly that calling to them was futile. Anyway, they'd abandoned him to this fearsome situation, so they could hardly be relied upon. Next was Mama Mia — a fervent and shrill invocation repeated rapidly over a 60- to 90-second interval.

By this time his shirt was off. The female relations were perspiring freely and beginning the fight to remove Tony's trousers. It was probably the threat of this indignity that induced Tony's ultimate and most prodigious initiative.

Struggling free of all three adults, he leaped partially clad in two bounds, first from the examining table to the floor, and then from the floor to the wall telephone. Grabbing the receiver, he put it to his ear and shouted, *"Police!"*

— DR. WILLIAM ROBERTSON

Details, Details

Acquiring life skills is an important part of the educational challenge all of us must endure. Some are born with a natural abundance of social graces, while others of us have to learn the hard way. When I was growing up, one didn't need a vast store of social savvy; life was simple. My real education began only when I found myself in the real world.

My first introduction to a drug salesman, predecessor of latter-day detail men and professional pharmaceutical representatives, was an experience so painful that I still wake up at night and cringe.

"Piper" McMillan, local baseball hero and representative of a national "drug house," was the first of what would turn out to be hundreds of representatives I would meet in the next 30 years, all with persuasive messages about the merits of the particular products manufactured by their respective companies.

I had the presence of mind to stand up when Piper came in and presented me with his card. I'd seen business cards in the movies but never actually held one in my hand. There, engraved on his company's fancy card, were his name, address, and telephone number. His name I already knew, and I was not really interested in his address or his phone number, so what was I to do with the card?

"There's nothing I can do for you —
you are a duck."

Thoughtlessly I eyed the wastepaper basket, and with a deft flick of the wrist, I tossed a strike. As the card cartwheeled out toward home, the message suddenly came to me that there was something amiss about my behaviour. Grovelling in the messy basket for Piper's card, I fumed against my stupidity for having missed the lecture on business card filing. Since then a few of the rough edges of my persona have been worn away, so that now I think Piper would probably give me a B- in decorum.

In Piper's day we were always greedy for any free drug samples that he and his colleagues were prepared to leave with us. Over the years samples became less attractive because so many people had drug plans or the ubiquitous "Drug Card." I'm still refreshed by meeting new representatives and renewing acquaintances with the older, established members of the profession.

Recently a nightmare of a patient returned to see me for the fourth time. I had desperately been trying to avoid major pelvic surgery on this patient, for it surely would have been lethal to her. She had proudly — and I believe without exaggeration — proclaimed that she had undergone 46 operations, and she volunteered the information that she was on the waiting list to have some of her interphalangeal joints replaced. Her family physician jokingly told me that her orthopod was able to retire early, due in large part to the many operations our hapless patient had undergone. Because of her numerous orthopedic problems, the patient was grossly shrunken and stooped; she stood about four foot nothing.

Thankfully her presenting complaint was not surgical in nature, but was strongly suggestive of a urinary tract problem. Because of her disabilities and the practical problems associated with trying to get an appropriate urine specimen, I decided to treat her empirically. I quickly wrote out a prescription for nitrofurantoin and gave it to her.

As an afterthought, seized with the vision of the difficulty she would have just getting into a drugstore, I decided to see if I had any available samples. I was able to lay my hands on some, but by this time the patient had hobbled out of the office. I ran out into the hallway and stopped her before she got on the elevator.

Because she was so short, I had to hunker down on the floor in order to look her in the eye as I spoke. I hurriedly transferred the capsules from their bulky containers to a more manageable package and gave her directions to take one capsule twice daily.

"I'm afraid you'll have to wait, Mr. Proctor. The doctor thinks he's seeing another patient."

From above a deep voice added, "With food."

I looked up to find the Norwich Eaton medical representative, Dave Pout, smiling happily down upon the two of us.

"It does my heart good," he said, "to see a doctor on his knees giving out samples of Macrodantin."

All our efforts and the drug must have worked, for I haven't seen the patient since. Perhaps she's in the hospital having her knuckles replaced.

— DR. KEVIN TOMPKINS

Complete Guide to Smoking

Thirteen Surefire Ways to Quit

Smoking is one of the oldest of human habits. There's no conclusive evidence indicating exactly where and when it began, but most scholars of antiquity agree that smoking even predates the practice of putting the forefinger between the lips and moving it rapidly up and down.

Archaeologists have discovered fossilized cigarettes and cigarette coupons dating back to Neolithic times. In Spain there are cave paintings showing men taking a cigarette break while hunting buffalo. Smoking was one of the most popular pastimes in classical Greece, despite Demosthenes' insistence that sucking on small pebbles was more enjoyable. The Huns under Attila invented the first cigar. And everyone knows the story of how Sir Walter Raleigh introduced tobacco to England but had trouble getting the practice off the ground because matches wouldn't be invented for over 100 years.

From its inception smoking was considered a pleasure, which explains why it has traditionally been thought of as harmful or wicked. During recent years, however, medical research has provided convincing evidence that smoking is at least as dangerous to one's health as giving mouth-to-mouth resuscitation to a werewolf.

In addition to the diseases mentioned on the outside of cigarette packs, smoking has been linked to a number of lesser known but

*"When I said it was a terminal malfunction,
I meant the computer, Mr. Larkin, not you."*

equally noxious conditions, including: chapped tongue, kippered uvula, fish lip, cirrhosis of the palate, rickety nerves, insomnambulism (inability to stay asleep while sleepwalking), bad dreams, bad shaves, shreds of tobacco in the navel, wheezing while pronouncing five-syllable words, jitters, acquisition of kitsch ashtrays, craving for snacks that taste like a terrier's foot, compulsion to use a roll-on deodorant on the tongue, shortness of breath, shortness of bad breath, spontaneous expectoration, unsightly carpet, laminated appearance, plaid fever, snake eyes, difficulty in leaping hydrants, enjoyment of rust, grout mouth, ashes in the lap, carbonated sputum, creaking gait, compulsion to smell the lapels, and corrugated sensations.

In the interest of public health here are 13 different methods of giving up smoking:

- Smoke only the cheapest brands of Burmese, Lithuanian, or Ugandan cigarettes. Their taste, which is usually something like a cross between garlic and marzipan, will undermine your enthusiasm for smoking.
- Whenever you feel the urge to smoke, take an ice cube tray out of the freezer and press your lips to its bottom.
- Wear a boxing glove on one hand and a catcher's mitt on the other. Lighting a cigarette will be a problem analogous to threading a needle during a typhoon.

- Phase out by switching to nontobacco cigarettes, which you can make yourself from a variety of unpalatable ingredients, such as vacuum cleaner dross, sawdust, confetti, cheesecloth, goldfish food, chicken feathers, material cleaned out of watch bands, freeze-dried coffee crystals, Astroturf, chopped pine needles, dried wine lees, regurgitated cat hairballs, belladonna, cellophane, dried seaweed, used flypaper, barbershop floor sweepings, shredded rubber bands, leaf mould, chopped-up runners' sweat-bands, peeling wallpaper, toadstools, ground-up Odor-Eaters from Salvation Army store shoes, et cetera. Use your imagination!
- Move to Commonwealth Bay, George V Coast, Antarctica, the windiest place in the world, where gales reach 300 kilometres per hour, and take an outside job.
- Destroy your taste buds. This can be done easily and inexpensively with a wood-burning kit or an adze.
- Spend several days in British Columbia or northern Ontario on a fireline fighting a major forest fire.
- Have someone slam a door on your lips.

"Yes, what is it? I'm very busy . . ."

- Phase out smoking by making it an annoyance. Only allow yourself to smoke when it's inappropriate, such as while shaving, taking a shower, playing basketball, dancing, extracting semen from a bull, hanging from the ceiling in gravity-inversion boots, tobogganing, having your teeth cleaned at the dentist's, et cetera.
- Make sure there's always half an inch of gasoline in all your ashtrays.
- Move to Mount Waialeale, Kauai, Hawaii, which has the world's record for the most rainy days per year — up to 350 — and take an outside job.
- Whenever you feel the urge to smoke, do something else equally pleasurable, like cleaning out the exhaust pipe of your car with your tongue.
- Remove all the cigarettes from every pack you buy, select one at random from each pack, carefully remove half the tobacco from it, and replace it with a generous amount of black gunpowder, then refill the cigarette with tobacco. Mix it with the others and return them all to their packs and smoke them at your normal rate. The combination of suspense, tension, and pyrotechnics should cure you of smoking.

— LARRY TRITTEN

PART THREE

In the Operating Room

My Vasectomy

The Unknown Future

The Research Committee had completed the business on the regular agenda and the conversation had switched to another scientific matter, namely a recent report on the long-term effects of vasectomy on adult male white Wistar rats. Unaccountably, some two years after the surgery, in a significant number of animals there had been a marked reduction in testicular size, and in three rodents the organs had simply disappeared.

Now a rat year is roughly equivalent to 15 human years, and Dr. V — was speculating darkly about the possibility of similar effects occurring in humans 20 to 30 years after being snipped. Unobtrusively I slipped my right hand into my trouser pocket and carefully fingered my globes. I breathed a sigh of relief and my facial tic, which always starts when I'm tense, stopped. They were still there — at least for now.

The discussion dimmed to my ears as my mind wandered back 20 years when I submitted myself to the sterilizing knife . . . Having reached the relatively advanced age of 35, I'd believed

*"I only just made it before
my Dad's vasectomy."*

that my emotional and material attrition was at an end, since the destructive proclivities of my children, aged 11, 10, and eight and a half, had all but waned. I was therefore stunned when, early in 1970, my wife announced that she was "two months gone."

In the weeks that followed, as my black despair lifted, I awoke to the fact that the "rhythm method" was simply too risky. It was then that I took the irrevocable decision to get myself chopped.

Two weeks later my wife and I put our case to a local surgeon who was known to be kindly disposed toward "male mutilation." As it turned out, my imitation of Uriah Heap proved superfluous. The interview was brisk and businesslike.

After satisfying himself that we were both in favour of the operation, he spelled out why, in his hands, it would be irreversible. He intended to resect two centimetres or so of vas on each side, then evaginate and suture the cut ends. Finally he intended to bury them as far apart as possible.

The chances of reanastomosis (spontaneous or otherwise) were, according to him, about as likely as finding the proverbial needle in a haystack (statistically about a million to one). It sounded just the sort of operation I needed. The interview was followed by a brief physical examination, and a date was set for two weeks later.

As we prepared to leave, our interviewer coughed apologetically and sheepishly produced a nondescript piece of paper. "A mere formality," he said, preempting my unspoken question. "Perhaps you and your wife would be so good as to sign here." X marked the spot.

Utterly out of character, since I never read anything remotely official-looking, I skimmed the words. One paragraph stood out: "The success of the operation cannot be guaranteed; in the event of pregnancy the surgeon will not be held liable."

He smiled reassuringly. "Just one of those irksome but necessary legalisms. I didn't bother until a colleague who used to do simply 'cut-and-tie,' not 'resect-evaginate-suture-and-bury,' was sued by a patient whose wife became pregnant. He's now in a psychiatric hospital." I signed meekly.

"I hope he knows what he's doing," my wife commented on the way out.

Two weeks later I drove the 18 miles to the hospital and presented myself for admission to the day ward. I fully expected to be homeward bound no later than 4:00 p.m. that afternoon.

My particulars were taken by a smiling, motherly head nurse who showed me to a two-bed alcove at the end of the main ward. Briskly I undressed, donned my new pajamas — special for the occasion — and jumped onto my bed. The other occupant, who turned out to be the Reverend Smailes, B.A., B.Div., nodded a welcome and then launched into his medical history. Since his case was more complicated than mine and would involve more than a minor cutting job, a general anesthetic had been recommended to minimize postoperative edema.

My own reasons for insisting on "oblivion," ostensibly similar, were altogether more devious. During my intern days as an ace circumciser, I'd invariably winced behind my mask as the penis was pulled through the operating slit, appearing like a tranquillized worm reluctant to leave its hole. I was convinced that the knowing winks and sly nudges that passed between the nurses were belittling.

Indeed, on one occasion when a particularly wizened specimen had appeared, I'm almost sure I heard the head nurse blow a faint but recognizable raspberry. I swore that if ever misfortune struck and my organ had to be laid out on a surgical platter for the world to see, a general anesthetic would be mandatory. You can be quite certain that this had nothing to do with post-traumatic edema.

"Dr. Simpkins, this is supposed to be an arthrodesis, not a scrimshaw!"

To the best of my knowledge the surgery went smoothly enough, and as I returned to the ward I glimpsed, through a rapidly lightening anesthetic haze, the Reverend Smailes on his way to the operating room. My penis and testes, covered by what seemed to be acres of insulating wool and crepe bandage, felt as big as a football. Relief flooded me: at any rate, they were still there.

I felt remarkably perky, and some 45 minutes later was indulging myself with coffee and cookies. Into my third cup I noticed that the ecclesiastic had returned, still very much under the influence of the anesthetic. It was clear that he lacked my amazing recuperative powers.

By 2:00 p.m., some four hours after the operation, I was testing my legs — waddling up and down the ward like an old-time sailor (because of the "football" between my thighs). I felt surprisingly well and estimated my time of departure as no later than 4:00 p.m. The reverend, I noted, had come around but looked anything but sprightly; he would certainly not be going home the same day.

I dressed myself, packed my pajamas, and announced my imminent departure to the head nurse.

"Has your wife arrived already?" she inquired.

"My wife?" I countered feebly. "Oh, no, I'm driving myself."

Her smile froze and, remarkably quickly for such a bulky woman, she moved to block the door. "You are under the influence of a general anesthetic and you must remain overnight."

Beginning to realize my fatal error, I said, "But surely that's for ordinary patients, Nurse. I feel tip-top and quite capable of driving my car 18 miles."

Obstinately she stood her ground and hissed through compressed lips, "Rules are rules and without permission you don't leave this hospital."

Becoming slightly irritated, I reaffirmed my competency and offered to sign myself out.

What until then had been a comparatively friendly exchange took a turn for the worse with the appearance of the nursing supervisor — Iron Cross and all — making her daily rounds. Singly they were formidable enough; together, it would be a walkover. I swallowed resignedly.

The cleric, who by now had recovered sufficiently to be sitting in a chair, was beginning to take some interest in the proceedings, as were several other patients who were attracted by the raised voices. Confronted by two members of the nursing profession apparently determined to prevent me from leaving, I became equally determined to do just that. All semblance of logic and reason disappeared, and in an increasingly loud and agitated manner, I began to insist on my rights.

The impasse was broken by the appearance of the anesthesiologist, who entered the ward briskly, Ku Klux Klan-like in his gown, eyes glittering behind his spectacles.

My heart sank. His dander was up and it seemed unlikely that I'd win him over. However, I made one last attempt. Insisting in a high-pitched voice that I was cerebrating as well as he was, I challenged him to put his money where his mouth was and to assess my psychomotor function formally. I distinctly remember yelling at him, "Go on then, test me! Anything you like."

My histrionic outburst provided all the necessary ammunition, and he delivered his coup de grace: "If you try to leave this hospital against my advice, I'll detain you under Section 30 of the Mental Health Act."

I couldn't believe my ears. Surely he was bluffing. He wouldn't dare. A psychiatrist outpsyched by an anesthesiologist! Calmer, I tried one last time. "I am not under the influence of —"

I got no further. My adversary's eyes had focused on another target. The reverend, who'd been perking up nicely, had suddenly ceased to take any further interest in our dispute. Deathly pale, head lolling on his chest, he was slowly, but with dignity, sliding down the chair to the floor.

"My God!" the anesthesiologist cried. "Delayed shock."

His eyes swivelled triumphantly to my stricken face. Instinctively I rushed forward, "football" and all, and, grunting with effort, heaved the collapsed cleric onto his nearby bed.

I prefer to think it was the Christian in me, but subconsciously it was more likely a last desperate attempt to convince the hostile trio that I was both mentally and physically 100 percent. But it was to no avail.

The anesthesiologist held out his hand. "The keys, if you please," he ordered.

"The keys?" I stammered. "What are you talking about?"

"The keys to your car — you can have them tomorrow when your tissues have been cleared of the dope."

I ground my teeth in impotent rage and the words choked in my throat. Argument was clearly fruitless. I was beaten. With bad grace I handed over the keys, which were deposited for safekeeping with a smirking head nurse.

Suddenly, as if by a flash of lightning, the idea came. James Bond-like, I would start the car by connecting the ignition wires beneath the dash. My lips curved slightly as I contemplated this soon-to-be-savoured triumph. Sneaky and underhanded it might be, but what a counterstroke! I might have lost every skirmish, but the campaign was mine.

I was so smugly absorbed with my thoughts that nurse's brief phone call went unnoticed. She replaced the receiver and turned to me brightly. "The ambulance will be here in ten minutes."

My grin became a *risus sardonicus*. "The ambulance?" I stammered. "I'm not going home in an ambulance. Don't forget. I'm staying here for the next 24 hours."

"There's been a change of plan," she told me, smirking. "Not home, just to the station. We must make sure you're safely on your train."

"Is it a rejection or a sneeze?"

I've never really gone for ESP, but since the station was clearly visible from my hospital window, and was less than 300 metres away, I began to wonder. Was it possible that she'd read my thoughts and had forestalled me? There was something in her smile that made my question unnecessary.

The ambulance duly arrived and I waddled into it. Three minutes later a hawk-eyed driver supervised me as I bought my ticket. God, I was mad!

I arrived at our station, some six miles from my village, at dusk. The temperature had dropped sharply and my cotton jacket (for the car journey) was not the best of protection. Shivering, I called home, and 15 minutes later my wife arrived to pick me up.

Whether or not my unexpected exposure to the elements had anything to do with it, I don't know, but by the next morning I was in the early throes of influenza.

Two weeks later, during convalescence, I retraced my steps to pick up the car.

"Oh, it's yours, Doctor," the hospital porter said. "We were just about to have it towed away."

I was brought back to the present abruptly. As if with one pair of eyes, the other members of the committee were staring at me with openmouthed incredulity. I followed their gaze

*"Well, Dorothy, it started out innocently enough
with a total hip replacement. Then it was a total shoulder,
elbows, wrists, knees, iron lung . . .
Next thing you know, I'm a tin man!"*

down to my inguinal region. A barely perceptible rotatory movement was apparent (to me and no doubt to them) in the vicinity of my right groin. It was my pocketed hand.

"Are you playing with yourself?" they asked challengingly. I gulped, smiled weakly, and stammered, "I suppose, in a manner of speaking, yes. But it's research," I added gamely. Their snigger was derisive.

— DR. A. J. COOPER

Placenta Previa

Although the heterosexual proclivity of the English has been recently questioned by a French prime minister, an experience I had while a midder clerk (obstetrics student) at St. George's

Hospital Medical School in London, England, would suggest that the British do indeed have not only what it takes but also a deserved reputation for dry humour.

In the 1970s the presence of a father in the delivery room was a relatively uncommon occurrence, but on this occasion a young Cockney father was invited to the birth of his first child. Dressed all in greens, he vacillated, rushing from the head of the table to the stirrups. With shrieks of joy from all, the infant was born and the senior registrar congratulated the father on the birth of a healthy child.

Father was most appreciative of the medical attention afforded his wife but asked to speak privately to the physician. Clearly he was very anxious.

Taking the senior registrar to a corner of the delivery room, he asked in all sincerity, "Well, Doc, when can me and the missus have sex again?"

The senior registrar looked first at the father and then at the mother, still in stirrups, and quietly informed him, "Sir, we usually wait until after the delivery of the placenta."

— DR. ANTHONY ATKINSON

Economics 101

Bodies, Boots, and Bondage

Extensive medical research has shown that if you were to place all the economists in the world end to end, they would never reach a conclusion. It has also been known for some time that if you were to place five economists in a room and ask them to solve a problem, you'd get a minimum of six answers.

All economists are now required to have one arm amputated at birth. This is to stop them from constantly saying that they're 100 percent certain that their advice is "The Right Answer to Life, the Universe, and Everything" — and then immediately qualifying it with: "But, on the other hand . . ." Beware of ambidextrous economists. Learn from *The Fugitive:* follow the one-armed man!

Economics, "the dismal science," has brought us some truly wonderful benefits: the depression, junk bonds, the collapse of communism, and the fall of the Marx brothers. Powerful stuff indeed!

An oft-quoted cliché is that the only certainties in life are death and taxes. It doesn't matter whether it's income tax, property tax, tire tax, or Big Mac attacks; you're still certain to end up with less and less income. The more gross it gets, the less you net. What can you do about it? How can you maximize your income? Economics 101 tells you how to get ahead in the age of Clintonomics.

Although it's illegal to buy and sell kidneys, they're not without value. The law deprives potential donors of income. Given the symmetrical redundancy of paired organs, we could get by with only one kidney, one adrenal, one eyeball, one gonad, et cetera. By not selling redundant organs, we're all incurring opportunity costs. An opportunity cost is whatever else you could have done with that dollar you blew on Blotto 649, beer, the rent, food, and other luxuries. In the case of a kidney, this is about U.S. $20,000.

The potential *recipients* are also disadvantaged by the law: demand currently exceeds supply, with an estimated demand of 12,000 kidneys per year and a supply of only 8,000 in the U.S. Thus kidney donors are losing $160 million per year (8,000 × $20,000). If donors really did receive $20,000 each for their kidneys, then the 4,000-kidney shortfall would also be made up, amounting to a further loss of $40 million (4,000 × $20,000), for a total of $200 million.

The recipient appears at first sight to gain from the law, in that the 8,000 recipients lucky enough to get kidneys save $160 million by not having to pay for them. However, the 4,000 potential recipients who don't receive kidneys lose. In practice, at least in the U.S., recipients tend to receive donated kidneys on the basis of ability to pay, rather than as gifts as intended by law. Many recipients end up paying most of the $20,000 real market price, anyway — not to the donors but to hospitals and middlemen.

Emmanuel Thorne and Gilah Langner reported in the *New York Times* that some U.S. hospitals were performing almost 30 percent of kidney transplants on foreigners who were allowed

to jump the queue over U.S. citizens because surgeons and hospitals could charge them nearly twice as much as they charged Americans.

So you can see that bodies can be big business. And in the business world there are really only three ways to get ahead — to obtain what business types call "competitive advantage." These are (1) Cost, (2) Focus, and (3) Differentiation.

Cost means being the cheapest guy in town for organs. This is an okay strategy in the short term, except that your competitors can easily copy you. If you cut the price of your spleen by 20 percent or start advertising 30 percent off or free if not delivered within one hour, or offer discount coupons for your adrenals, the competition can easily duplicate your strategy. Competition becomes fierce.

Ultimately the consumer/recipient benefits, because prices get lower and lower, but you, the producer/donor, lose out. You

"Light meat or dark?"

end up with a so-called "spoiled market," especially if you're left with lots of unsold merchandise and your freezer is full.

Focus is a much better bet. You specialize in, for example, corneas. You corner the cornea market. You get Yves St. Laurent or Frank Lloyd Wright's dog to develop a designer image and wonderfully expensive packaging and logos. You run TV commercials and slick ads in *Family Practice, Transplantation Review*, and *Cornea and Golf Digest*. You offer customers any colour of cornea they want, but use preposterous interior-designer terms such as "taupe" and "architectural yellow."

It's very difficult for competitors to clone your product, service, and style. Build up expertise and image, capitalize on the snob value of Calvin Klein corneas, and you're laughing all the way to the bank — assuming it's still there and didn't lend money to Olympia and York.

Differentiation means that you make your product or service different from the pack. You offer a complete computerized Home HLA Tissue Typing Service for recipients and donors. You specialize in after-graft service. You offer a five year buffer-to-buffer warranty on parts, labour, and formaldehyde.

Being different can be a very effective strategy for gaining sustainable competitive advantage. It can also get you on *Oprah Winfrey* between slots on "Gay Whales That Seduced/Married Jacques Cousteau Impersonators" and a mud-slinging match between estranged members of the American Association of Proposterous People Who Appear on Mindless Chat Shows and Make Complete Fools of Themselves.

On the macro scale the entire body is worth a great deal. Its scrap value is enormous. All those complex enzymes, DNA, and ribosomes could be recycled at great profit. Keep this in mind when you reach the end of your economic lifetime.

Economic lifetime is how many years something is worth keeping in terms of productivity rather than how long it would last physically. For physicians their physical life is perhaps 70 to 80 years, but their economic life is about 40 years, from residency to retirement.

Once you've been fully depreciated by your accountant and your economic life is over, don't burn up your body in an incinerator, or decompose it in the ground. Get green, be environmentally friendly and totally recyclable: sell your body to a biotech company. Why decay away in vivo when you could remain (in the main) in vitro?

Selling your body is not as lucrative as selling your mind or, rather, your imagination. Sex, like ice cream, comes in many different flavours. Vanilla sex generates tax-free income but carries considerable risk, not least from infection with HIV, gonorrhea, or syphilis.

Differentiation into the so-called high-end "Fetish/S&M but Strictly No Sex" market may be a solution. Working clothes are expensive but fully tax-deductible. Dressing *cap a pé* in black leather will cost around $1,000, including riding crop, boots, spurs, and an investment in some high-yield bondage stocks. Economist Karl Milton Keynes has demonstrated a strong correlation between fishnet earnings and gross length of boot; spiky, thigh-high, black patent leather boots yield, on average, 457.39 times more earnings than a pair of Dr. Scholl's orthopedic clogs (plus or minus three nonstandard deviations from normal). Earnings data for female call persons, wearing either kind of footwear, aren't currently available.

No matter how much you differentiate, focus, or cut your prices, in the end the Taxman Cometh for us all. Myron Bulrooney's replacement/clone and your local provincial clones/clowns will all want their cut. Tax forms and regulations have become more complex and increasingly incomprehensible to all but the idiot civil savants who design them.

If income tax, the recession, or the GST are causing you depression, remember Winston Churchill's maxim: "Never despair." Try to keep things in perspective. Taxes and recessions are setbacks, but not tragedies. A tragedy is a busload of economists driving off a cliff — and there's one empty seat.

— DR. IAN WILKINSON

Oat Cuisine

After a man was admitted to a hospital in Connecticut last year complaining of abdominal pain, doctors removed a solid, two-foot-long piece of oat bran from his small intestine.

And we thought we were fed up with fibre!

Foxy Lady

In June 1951, on the very first day of my junior internship, I was placed on call in the delivery room. I'd witnessed a few deliveries before but had never participated in one. The senior intern admitted she knew little about obstetrics and hated the subject.

At approximately 10:00 p.m. a 200-pound-plus woman arrived in the department, screaming that her baby was coming fast. She was rushed to the nearest labour room, and ten minutes later one of the nurses came out and said to me, "Come quickly, Doctor. Something is abnormal!"

"I'm going to be late for vascular rounds.
I'm stuck in a major artery."

I looked frantically for the senior intern, but she'd conveniently vanished. When I reached the labour room, I found the patient half-undressed, lying on her back, and in between her two enormous thighs was an eight- to 10-inch-long black furry tail, soaked with amniotic fluid, apparently sticking out of the vagina.

I froze on the spot with fear. *What the hell is that?* I thought. Breaking into a sweat, I suddenly remembered something the professor had said: "If you ever see something abnormal, call me immediately."

That was all I needed. I rushed to the phone and called him up. When I described the situation, he thought I was pulling his leg. However, I insisted so much, adding that this was my first case and the senior intern was unavailable, that he agreed to come right away.

Quite relieved that help was on the way, I managed to calm down sufficiently to realize that the whole thing was crazy and impossible. I went back into the room, examined this would-be monstrosity more closely, and found out what it actually was. (Boy, I'd never felt so stupid before!)

When this lady had arrived in the department, she was wearing a fox fur collar, that had fallen beneath her as she'd lain down. Naturally the fur had gotten soaked when the amniotic sac ruptured.

Fortunately I was able to reach the professor before he left home, but you can imagine what happened when the other interns heard about this!

— DR. ROBERT BISSON

Shortnin' Up

Nowadays the ecologically advanced are very much for the preservation of trees, whales, and prepuces. I'm not sure why forswearing foreskin felling has become part of the greening of North America, but "shortening" now gets as bad a press as clear-cut logging.

Even in the bad old days when it was considered healthy, hygienic, wholesome, and he-mannish to sport a docked dink, some of the male babies escaped the chopping block. Unfortunately a few of these "uncircumcised" little boys would end up with problems soluble only by "the knife."

Little Johnny was a patient of mine whose phimosis had been allowed to reach the state where on voiding, a veritable balloon would develop before a fine, all-encompassing spray commenced. This would necessitate his wearing gumboots and a slicker if bladder-emptying was desired without an accompanying change of clothes. Mother finally got tired of mopping up and overcame her initial reluctance to risk her pride and joy to the vagaries of the scalpel.

She really was quite fearful, so that I was tempted to quote Shakespeare: "There's a destiny that shapes our end, rough-hew it how we will." However, I did manage to restrain my inner imp, and carefully explained the procedure to her.

Everything went well until, postoperatively, I heard a great scream from Johnny's room. He'd just awakened and pulled down his bedclothes to see why his thing was sore. The sight of the bloody bandage was too much for him. When I came in, he hollered, "Call my mom! Tell her they've killed it!"

I've always thought that the Hebrew tradition really carries out a circumcision with the ritual and ceremony it deserves. They use a great, awe-inspiring knife instead of a measly scalpel. Fuller's earth is used to stop any bleeding. A *mazel tov* toast is drunk to celebrate, and the sounding of the *shofur* notifies the world that a great deed has been done.

The best I've been able to do to add a little colour to our type of circumcision has been to sing a few bars of "Mammie's little baby loves shortnin', shortnin' / Mammie's little baby loves shortnin' up."

One day I was giving anesthetics for a great string of tonsillectomies. One little boy seemed unduly distressed, so I asked what the trouble was. "They're going to cut off my pee-pee!" cried the utterly devastated little guy. As this was in the days before patient-name wrist bands, this remark saved him from awakening with an awful sore throat, and everyone in the OR from even worse complications.

I did my best to console him, pointing out how we were only going to make it much trimmer, neater, and easier to use. He still wanted an old-fashioned, crude, rude, unadorned thing. Besides, I'm sure that he was secretly afraid that he was going to be turned into that most despised of creatures, *a girl!*

— DR. BRADLEY HOUSTON

A Brush with the Law

One's first job as an independent physician, perhaps like one's first sexual encounter, often produces an unusual mixture of memories: the pleasant and triumphant interspersed with the painful and embarrassing. One of the first locums I did after completing my internship provides a case in point.

It was a glorious summer in northern Ontario, and Thunder Bay was playing hose to the Canada Games. I ran a busy general practice, did lots of emergency room coverage, and even served as an on-site physician for some Canada Games events.

After several weeks and an untold number of lives saved and pills dispensed, the last day arrived. The GP I was replacing, and whose car I was using, was driving his camper with wife and kids all the way from Winnipeg that day. I was on call that night for ER from home. An hour or so before the camper arrived I was paged and told that a young man on a ten-speed bike had been hit by a car and was in ER with a compound fracture.

"Too bad we couldn't save the hand."

Jumping up, I dashed to the car and drove toward the hospital well in excess of the speed limit. An event that I'd often wondered about then took place as I spotted the flashing red lights of a police cruiser in my rearview mirror.

A certain Irish internist from my medical school days had suggested that the solution to this problem was to keep on speeding and wave your stethoscope at the pursuing officer as he overtook you. The only problem with this approach is that a quick-thinking officer might overtake you a second time, waving a pair of handcuffs.

So I dutifully pulled over, leaped out of the car in my jeans and T-shirt, and ran back to the cruiser looking particularly undoctorish. I did produce my stethoscope rather weakly as my badge of office, but the constable, still sitting in his vehicle, looked unimpressed. When I relayed the story of the unfortunate cyclist, the scene of whose accident the officer had just left, he grudgingly told me to go ahead. Like a knight in shining armour eager to save yet another life, I ran back to the GP's car to go the remaining eight blocks to the hospital. To my horror I discovered that I'd locked myself out of the car! Not only that, the lights were on and the engine was running!

The incredulous policeman pulled slowly up beside me and said simply, "You didn't." There followed an eight-block ride in a police cruiser with my face as red as the flashing lights overhead.

"Do you think maybe you could make just one small mistake? I need the money."

Once things were organized in the ER and I was heading to the OR to assist the orthopedist, my thoughts returned to the locked vehicle eight blocks away peacefully running out of gas. I called the GP, who'd just arrived home after driving all day with four particularly lively kids, and he was slightly less than thrilled when I asked him if he could retrieve his locked vehicle. I hadn't the heart to tell him it was still running.

The next morning, when I met the GP to do hospital rounds, he made little reference to the events of the previous evening. He offered to drive me to the airport in the same vehicle that had just had its "night on the town." And as we walked out of the hospital, he stopped at the front door and whistled as if calling a dog. In response to my puzzled look, he said that considering the way his car had been behaving recently, he thought it might answer his call and drive up to the hospital to pick us up.

— DR. RODERICK SYME

"What we propose to do is remove your head, have a look
inside your neck, and then close you up again.
It's a brand-new technique, and I must tell you that it
does involve certain dangers. The question
is: how badly do you want to get rid of that cough?"

Great Moments in Surgery

The risk of dying from surgery has dropped dramatically in this century. In Victorian times death was a routine outcome of many operations, and in one record-breaking amputation, a British surgeon managed to achieve a mortality rate of 300 percent.

Dr. Robert Liston practised in the mid-19th century in London's fashionable Mayfair district. He was famous, flamboyant, and vain, and his hallmark was speed.

In the days before anesthesia it was important to get the operation over with quickly. Even though Dr. Liston became the first surgeon in Europe to use anesthesia, which he referred to as a "Yankee dodge," he failed to appreciate that it made speed obsolete.

"Oh, how embarrassing! There's a woman over there wearing the same cosmetic surgery."

The normal procedure was for the patient to be sedated with morphia and as much alcohol as he could drink, then firmly strapped down. The surgeon would hold the "amputation knife," which was rather like a 10-inch kitchen knife, pointing toward himself with the blade facing down. He would pass the knife under the patient's leg and around as far as possible, cutting down to the bone in a single, rapid circular motion, known as the *coup de maître*.

Dr. Liston would announce the beginning of surgery with the cry, "Time me, gentlemen!" Then he would quickly perform the *coup de maître*, put the knife between his teeth, grab the saw, and hack through the bone. He would then tie off the artery with special forceps he had designed.

His best time for a leg amputation was two and a quarter minutes. However, his *coup de maître* was so powerful and sweeping that his unfortunate assistant, who was holding the leg, lost his fingers, and a spectator who was standing too close had his coattails cut. Although the spectator wasn't injured by the blade, the poor man was so frightened by the near miss that he had a heart attack and died on the spot.

Dr. Liston's wounded assistant subsequently died of hospital gangrene, which was not unusual in the days before antisepsis. The patient also succumbed to hospital gangrene.

That's the record — a 300 percent mortality rate — and given the advances in surgical procedures since Dr. Liston's day, it's likely to stand for some time.

— DR. JOHN COCKER

A Miracle Cure

Back in the mid-1950s, when medical training was more of an apprenticeship than it is today, there came a critical time in every student's career when he was let loose on a suspecting public.

I say "suspecting" because the hospital where I did my training, St. Bartholomew's in London, England, had always been a "free" hospital — at least since 1123 A.D., when the first records were made — and patients were very much aware of the fact that it was a medical school.

"Bad news and good news, Mrs. Fisk. It seems you got the wrong graft. But not to worry — it's taken beautifully."

The first overt surgical act that the student performed at St. Bartholomew's was the draining of hydroceles (a large cyst of the testicle). There was a cadre of aged, infirm men who would come to the out-patient department every few months. A student would apply a little local anesthetic to the scrotum and then insert a large-bore needle and drain out the straw-coloured fluid. All very satisfying.

The care and attention that the student devoted to this apparently simple procedure were inversely proportional to the number of times he had performed it. After he had half a dozen of them under his belt, so to speak, the whole thing took just a few moments and was carried out with the casual air of insouciance that befits the expert.

One day I was on duty when a little old man, bent forward at the waist, came limping in on the arm of a nurse. The two of us sat him on the table and carefully laid him back. As a veteran of the procedure, he waited with misplaced confidence, unaware of the miracle that was about to be performed.

His pants were pulled down, exposing his scrotum with a grapefruit-sized swelling. The skin of the scrotum was somewhat excoriated, even raw in places, but dermatology was still ahead in the medical curriculum.

The skin preparation used back then was cetavlon, a fine soapy solution, handy for washing cars as well as scrotums. It's out of fashion now — mainly, I think, because it's too cheap. On this particular day, however, the bottle was empty. So I looked around and found another skin preparation — ether. This volatile substance was sometimes used before giving injections. It's just as useless as alcohol but smells nice, and being incredibly flammable it discourages smoking, which means it can't be all bad.

Pouring a liberal amount of the ether into a dish, I dipped a swab into it and placed the dripping swab onto the excoriated skin of the scrotum. The effect was remarkable.

The little old man, formerly bent and crippled, straightened up, hit a high C, and cried, "Oo-oo-oo-oo!" He leaped off the table, pulled up his pants, and ran out of the room. Clutching his genitals, he disappeared with the speed of an athlete needing a steroid test, still wailing "Oo-oo-oo-oo," a sound that faded into the distance, like that of a police car driving away.

He was never seen again, and I have never since seen such an effective or rapid cure for arthritis.

— DR. JOHN COCKER

115

Misinformed Consent

As a junior surgical resident in Liverpool, I was once asked by my chief to a "minor" surgical list in the operating room adjoining his. One of the patients was a 15-year-old mentally retarded male booked in for circumcision at his mother's request.

The operation went smoothly enough, but in the post-operative period he developed a massive hematoma, giving his penis the appearance of a large grapefruit grasped in the hand of a small child. I like to think it was the patient's propensity for masturbation rather than any deficiency in surgical technique that resulted in this unfortunate complication.

The problem (like the penis) was handled aggressively from the outset, with the gamut of therapy ranging from surgical

"Understaffed? I've carried out five operations this morning and I'm only the janitor!"

drainage (difficult) to medicinal leeches (interesting). After a week's prostration and pain, the unlucky young man miraculously recovered and was limping out of the ward when I first met his mother and sister.

It appeared that the sister, who was two years younger than the patient, was also mentally retarded. In the course of my conversation with the mother, it became clear that the two of them had struck up an incestuous relationship.

"I know the boy suffered, Doc," the mother said, "but was the operation a success? Are you sure he won't have no babies?"

"Mrs. S., your son had a circumcision, not a vasectomy!"

"Damnit, that's the word I was looking for!"

— DR. BRIAN BOYD

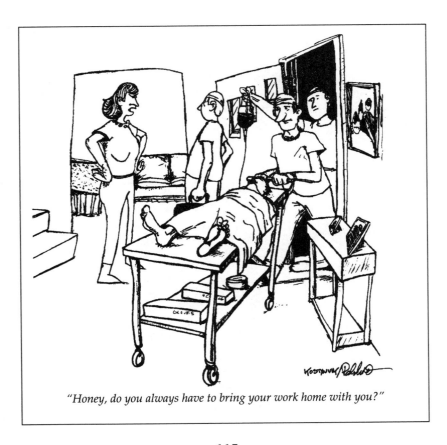

"Honey, do you always have to bring your work home with you?"

Clear Solids Only

During my first job as a house surgeon (junior intern), it was my lot to do the history and physical for a patient who was being investigated for constipation. I was pleased to find that she was a concise historian, answering my questions quite succinctly and without the usual ramblings and diversions. In short order I knew the length of time she'd had the problem, its severity, and the absence of any other associated symptoms.

Then I asked her, "Do you take anything to help?"

To my surprise, she replied, "Yes, broken glass."

I elected to ignore this for the moment and get on with the physical, which went very smoothly and without abnormality — until it came to the rectal examination, when I sustained a small laceration to my finger!

A subsequent flat plate of the abdomen showed the whole gut to be packed solid with shards of glass. Strangely enough, stools for occult blood were negative. The nursing staff confirmed that if any glass was left at this patient's bedside, it disappeared, although no one actually witnessed her eating it.

I never did discover the reason for her addiction to glass, as she was transferred to the psychiatric unit forthwith. My finger healed without incident.

— DR. BARBARA ROSTRON

"I'm afraid his stomach was the way to his heart."

The 58th Variety

One night about 10 years ago, while I was on duty in the Emergency Department of a Quebec City hospital, I was awakened by the nurse at 5:00 a.m. She wouldn't tell me on the phone the reason for the patient's visit, and I soon realized why: here he was, about 35 years old, six feet tall, 250 pounds, bleeding heavily from the anal region. The cause? He had put a junior-size Heinz fruit bottle in his anus, and it had slipped into his rectum, where it was now stuck.

The surgeon that I woke up didn't believe my story at first, and he had a good reason not to: it was April 1.

In the operating room all the surgeon's efforts were in vain. Finally he asked that someone get the forceps from the delivery room. Then he put the forceps in the rectum and delivered the bottle!

But the story doesn't end there. The Quebec medical insurance board refused to pay for this "April 1 bottle delivery" at the standard delivery rate. Only when it had received the operation protocol did the board agree to pay this surgeon the delivery rate.

The patient was sent for psychiatric treatment. Four years later, guess who appeared at 2:00 a.m.! Right! Same patient, now divorced, but with a different problem this time — he'd put a . . . in his . . . But that's another story.

— DR. JEAN LAVALLEE

On the High Seas

Some years ago I accepted a temporary position as a ship's doctor on a cruise ship in the Mediterranean. It was a tough job, but somebody had to do it. Blue skies, blue sea, 7,000-calorie meals with snacks, all free! And, to top it all, I was being paid.

Then, without warning, the fear that hunts all ship's doctors became a reality: someone actually became ill! And not just anyone. It was a vital member of the crew — the laundryman.

A ship can manage quite well without the captain, or the mate, or even the doctor, but there's no way it can get by without the laundryman. If the officers don't have clean, crisp shirts to wear, authority collapses and anarchy prevails.

It was a crisis.

On a cruise ship the members of the crew live in a part of the vessel that's never seen by the passengers, nor by the light of day. It's way, way down in the bowels of the ship, about a centimetre from the ocean depths. It's a hot, smelly place where you couldn't get a licence to keep laboratory rats. I suspect there were some unlicensed rats, but I tried not to look.

In this hellhole, on a bottom bunk, lay the laundryman, who was Chinese. The light was dim, but I could see that he was ill.

Even early on in my medical career I could usually tell if someone was ill. I might not know why, or how, but "ill" was a diagnosis I could make with some confidence.

The patient knew no more English than I knew Chinese. However, I've found in my travels that there are certain words that are universal. Among them are *okay, kaput, nix* and, oddly enough, *picnic*. Using these, I tried to find out what was wrong.

Help was offered by the gallery of spectators that had quickly appeared, pushing and shoving to get a good view. "He sick," they suggested. "He chuck up."

Armed with this history and my universal words, I began the examination. All became clear when I got to the abdomen, which was rigid, boardlike, just as our teachers had told us, even in the 1950s.

Back in Canada the next step would have been simple. Call an ambulance, whisk the patient off to hospital, and get back home for dinner. On the high seas it isn't quite so easy.

We were due in Cyprus the next day. I had two litres of IV fluid of unknown vintage, with foreign writing on it and a slight sediment. I'm still not sure what I should have done.

What I did do was give 15 milligrams of morphia subcutaneously, gave the patient some ice water, and observed him every hour or so. His general condition seemed stable, so I held off the doubtful IV fluid and continued with the morphia, as required, hoping his omentum was sealing off the perforation.

"And a little less power on the laser scalpel, please, Nurse."

My confidence grew as we approached Cyprus, but then I was shattered by an announcement that due to bad weather we were changing course and heading for Alexandria, three days away. This news called for a quick trip to see the Greek captain. I explained the situation, with the help of sign language, and some radio calls were made to the shore.

Before very long, with 800 passengers watching, the captain made a very clever manoeuvre in the choppy sea. Putting on full rudder and reversing the engines, he slewed the ship sideways, creating a patch of flat, sheltered water on the lee side. Into this patch a Royal Navy landing vessel came alongside, and the ailing laundryman was transferred.

To prepare the patient, I'd organized a stretcher, got all his clothes together, and written a detailed account of all that I'd done for him, including the times I'd given morphia, et cetera. I put this account in an envelope marked, "To the Doctor," and pinned it to the front of his pajamas.

As the Royal Navy vessel came alongside, the two ships kissed momentarily, the stretcher was transferred and I, for one, breathed a genuine sigh of relief. The passengers cheered as I shook hands with the captain.

Minutes later I settled into my usual chair at the bar, where I could watch the sexual shenanigans of the younger passengers. I was still basking in the afterglow of one who knows he has taken part in a real-life drama with a happy ending, when a white-clad waiter arrived with a silver tray.

What could it be? A congratulatory bottle of champagne? A letter from an admirer? No, it was my slightly scruffy envelope marked, "To the Doctor."

— DR. JOHN COCKER

Oops!

Years ago, among my patients, was a pleasant lady named Gert MacDougall. Always cheerful and bubbly, she and her husband ran a small convenience store where I often stopped on my way home from work.

Unfortunately, at age 65 or so, she developed cervical cancer and underwent a course of radium and X-ray treatments. I'd see her on a regular basis after that, and I remember that each time she came, she'd bring me a package of candy as a small gift.

One day, while I was in the middle of a surgical procedure at the hospital, a nurse came in with a message for me that a Mrs. Gert MacDougall was bleeding, and quite heavily. My instructions were for her to get to the hospital immediately, where she would be brought to the minor OR examination room for pelvic assessment.

I was pleased to hear, as I was finishing the skin sutures on my patient, that Mrs. MacDougall had arrived and was awaiting me in the exam room, already up "in stirrups."

I moved to the other room, greeted her with usual warmth, and asked whether there was a lot of bleeding.

Her answer: "I was standing over the sink doing the dishes when all of a sudden the blood started to drip from my nose and it hasn't stopped since!"

To which my comment was that forbidden OR word, "Oops!"

— DR. N. K. MACLENNAN

*"I've had a very rewarding day — four heart operations,
two hips, and a kidney. And to think I nearly went into medicine instead of law."*

Wearing the Mantle

Labels are important. King, queen, president, prime minister, premier, chairman. All very grand indeed. The possessor of such a label is no longer a mere human; public adulation and ceremony raise him above the common herd. Wisdom and competence are not to be questioned because these qualities are bestowed upon the individual by the label.

Labels are important in medicine. Without a label we have no authority whatsoever. With the appropriate title we enjoy almost unparalleled privilege. Again, competence and wisdom are guaranteed by the label. Postgraduate training programs are testimony to this truth.

For instance, a resident undergoing training in internal medicine will rotate through many subspecialties. From the first day of his rotation on, say, cardiology, he will often be the first, particularly during antisocial hours, to consult on patients on other services who have problems of the heart. He will bring with him the authority of his new office, and competence will be assured: "Cardiology has seen the patient" — and the patient will then move on to gastroenterology.

When, on the first day of his new rotation, the resident sees a patient with diarrhea on the cardiology service, a note is made: "Gastroenterology has seen the patient."

An interesting epiphenomenon also occurs the moment the resident leaves a given service — he's no longer deemed competent because he no longer wears the mantle of that particular specialty. Hence the anomaly whereby the resident who has completed his training in cardiology is asked by his new consultant in gastroenterology to obtain a cardiology opinion, only to find that the opinion is rendered by the resident who has just left gastroenterology to start his rotation in cardiology.

Instant authority and competence were bestowed upon me in the manner just described when I was undertaking surgical training in Britain. I'd completed several years of general surgery and the head was the only part of the human body that I hadn't hitherto invaded. I therefore elected to do six months of neurosurgery. I was three days into my new job when my consultant, Mr. B. (surgeons in Britain are called Mr. rather than Dr.), a short-statured, volatile, and abrasive South African, decided for the first time in his life to take Saturday afternoon off to watch his son run in the school sports day.

Fifteen minutes into sports day and I (i.e., Neurosurgery) was called to the Emergency Department to see a young man who'd fallen off a mountain in Scotland. He was hypotensive and deeply unconscious. After the infusion of copious amounts of fluid, his blood pressure was restored and his urine output reestablished. However, he showed no signs of waking up.

At this point I reminded myself that my mandate and area of competence were no longer a torn liver or spleen but the young man's head, which was none too responsive. I therefore assumed the mantle of Neurosurgical Competence and began to consider such things as extradural and subdural hematomata.

It just so happened that I'd been reading in the bath that morning my new book, *A Handbook of Neurosurgery: A Guide for Beginners,* written by an aggressive Australian neurosurgeon who'd had considerable experience with the Flying Doctor

Service. I recalled three points very clearly. First, making burr holes is a minor neurosurgical procedure and one shouldn't be put off because one is dealing with somebody's head. Second, when in doubt, make a hole. Third, drill low.

So I announced to the Emergency Room sister with considerable aplomb that I would perform an emergency burr hole. She first begged my pardon. When I repeated my intention, a blank look crossed her face, followed by a dark frown. This should have been my first clue that my course of action was inappropriate.

Sensing the sister's antipathy, I decided that I needed to take a firm hand and explained that this was a life-and-death situation and that life was rapidly departing from the shattered carcass on the table. With a steady voice I asked that she send over to the neurosurgical theatre for trephines (a surgical cutting instrument), Hudson brace, et cetera.

Five minutes later an ashen-faced theatre sister arrived carrying a tray of instruments. "Have you taken leave of your senses?" she hissed. I hadn't had the opportunity of meeting this good lady before.

"No, Sister, but I'm afraid that the senses appear to have left this patient."

"Ever been on TV before?"

"What do you think Mr. B. is going to say when he hears about this?" she retorted.

"I am afraid, Sister, that Mr. B. isn't here at the moment to say anything." She clearly needed some encouragement, so I went on, rather pompously, "We need to exclude a reversible intracranial lesion as quickly as possible." I then proceeded to drill into the side of the patient's head and was jubilant to find a bulging dura. "Aha!" I said. "Subdural hematoma."

My triumph was short-lived, however, as on opening the dura I was greeted by a protruding temporal lobe. Not to be deterred by the embarrassed shuffling of feet as other people left the room, I turned the patient's head and drilled low into the other side. Again, a bulging temporal lobe.

"Well, Sister, nobody can say we denied this patient the right to life," I said in as sunny a tone as I could muster.

"We?" she snorted as she stomped out of the department, clutching her tray of precious tools.

A subsequent CAT scan showed massive cerebral edema and intracerebral contusions that, unfortunately, were not reversible.

It was sometime later — and later than I expected — that I received a message from the switchboard to call Mr. B. at home. Apparently he'd received a blow-by-blow account of the afternoon's events from the theatre sister and had gone home to rest. I could detect a tremor in his otherwise cold and controlled voice.

"I have been a neurosurgeon for 30 years," he said, "and I have never carried out burr holes in the Emergency Department. You have been here three days, and not only have you carried out burr holes, but you have carried out *bilateral* burr holes."

Mr. B. had had a heart attack only a few months earlier and still experienced chest pains with little provocation. Not wishing to be responsible for a recurrence of his illness, I decided to defuse the situation by not attempting to explain my activities in the Emergency Room. I told him that I hoped his son had won his race at school, that I hoped we would not be quite so busy for the rest of the weekend, and that I was looking forward to joining him for our first elective list together on Monday morning.

I was very happy six months later to regain my previous label:
General Surgeon (with No Special Competence in Neurosurgery).

— DR. JOHN GATELY

My First Patient

It is now almost 50 years since I commenced my medical studies at King's College, University of London, England. In those days my parents were living in a small village north of London, and I commuted daily by train.

Within a short period I had the good fortune to meet a family also from the same village. There were the widowed mother, a son, and two very attractive daughters named Isabel and Yvonne. From that point onward they all took a keen interest in my progress and encouraged me in my efforts.

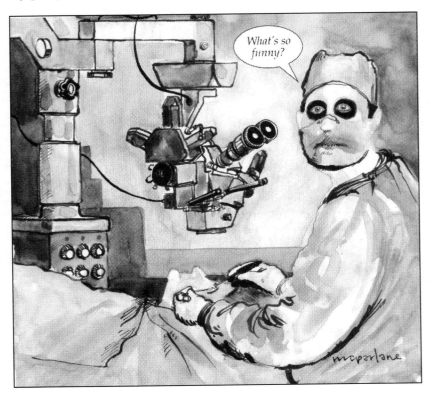

127

The years of study passed, and then the finals were upon me. After sitting them, I had to wait a while before the results were announced. Then I travelled up to London where I found I had successfully graduated. The rest of the day was mine, and I suddenly realized that, for a short time at least, I was a "gentleman of leisure" with absolute freedom to do as I chose.

My decision was to return home immediately to tell my parents and those friends who had so consistently encouraged me that I had now graduated as a physician. After informing my parents of the good news, I walked down the road to the house of these friends, having first taken the precaution of placing my stethoscope prominently in the outside pocket of my overcoat!

I reached the house, walked up the driveway, and knocked on the door. There was some delay before the mother came to the front door, and when she appeared, she looked somewhat worried. She still seemed subdued even as I gave her the news of my graduation. Finally she said, "So now you are a fully fledged doctor and can treat patients."

I assured her that this was correct.

She remained silent for a further minute and then said, "Isabel is still at work, but Yvonne has had a tummy upset and looseness and came home early from work today."

I hastened to assure her that in my new capacity I could prescribe something to relieve the discomfort.

"It's not as simple as that," she replied. "After Isabel and Yvonne left for work this morning, I decided to revarnish the bathroom toilet seat with a special fast-drying varnish. Unknown to me, Yvonne came home early from work, picked up a favourite magazine, adjourned to the bathroom, and sat herself down on the toilet seat for an extended stay. Now she cannot get off it and appears to be lodged there permanently."

Then she wished to know if I had ever encountered such a problem previously. Up to that time such a clinical situation had not come my way, either through my reading, Emergency Department experience, or hospital rounds. However, it seemed wiser not to commit myself to a clear and unequivocal admission of ignorance, so I took refuge in a noncommittal reply, indicating that these problems did occur from time to time even in the best-regulated households.

I wanted to laugh, but it was obvious that, at all costs, I had to preserve a straight face and serious professional demeanour. However, within this context a certain amount of private levity was permissible, and I silently reviewed a series of possible options for treatment:

- Blasting powder and gelignite. This option was dismissed immediately. My friendship with Yvonne and the rest of the family could not possibly survive such drastic therapy. I further realized that I, an impecunious newly qualified doctor, would be liable for the costs of a new bathroom along with the possible medical-legal complications associated with the physical and mental trauma sustained by the patient. In more senses than one it would be difficult to keep such therapy quiet, and my reputation would hardly be enhanced.
- Blowtorch therapy. Equally unsuitable for the reasons given above.
- Mallet and wedge-shaped wooden block. A few deft strokes might separate the patient from the varnish, while undoubtedly separating me from the goodwill of the family.

- Disarticulation of the toilet seat. This would certainly get the patient out of the bathroom. However, her return to work would present problems, for even if suitable clothing were to be found, a variety of questions from the curious could prove to be especially embarrassing.
- Sandpaper. Too rough on all concerned.
- Nail polish remover. Used with care and discretion, this could be the treatment of choice.

The mother confirmed that there was plenty of nail polish remover available, and after obtaining some, she led the way to the bathroom. She looked inside and confirmed that her daughter was still there, enthroned and firmly trapped. I introduced myself and, discreetly averting my eyes, remained outside the bathroom.

In order to break the ice, Yvonne and I spent a few minutes discussing the weather. Then mother went to work with the nail polish remover while I remained nearby giving technical advice.

Fortunately the procedure was working, and from time to time there was a sharp indrawing of breath as the firmly planted bottom was peeled away from the toilet seat. Finally I heard the exultant tones of the mother: "Stand up, Yvonne. You're free, you're free!" This was followed by the sounds of triumphant plumbing. All that remained was to recommend a suitable soothing cream for the affected skin.

The ordeal was over. My reputation had been established, our friendship had been preserved and, apart from the need to revarnish the toilet seat, no structural damage had been sustained to the bathroom fixtures.

The mother and I then adjourned to the drawing room, where I received her thanks and was offered afternoon tea with scones, Devonshire cream, and strawberry jam. While we were waiting for Yvonne, we had another discussion about the weather before the mother broached the subject of my professional charges for the advice and treatment provided. I hastened to assure her that I was ever mindful of her earlier kindnesses and that, of course, there would be no charge.

Yvonne then entered the room. She was perfectly composed and made no reference to the previous incident. I noted, however, that she sat on two cushions!

*It was only after he'd reported his wallet stolen
that Arnold first noticed his spleen was also missing.*

The intervening years have brought great changes for both of us. At that time I had no idea that the restrictions and frustrations of the British National Health Service would oblige me to look elsewhere for opportunities in medical practice and cause me to emigrate to Canada. For her part, Yvonne married and presented her husband with two fine sons.

Notwithstanding these developments, we have maintained a constant friendship across the years, and when I return to England on vacation, I make a point of visiting her. When we meet, I ask her if she is keeping well. Nothing else is said, our eyes meet, and even after all this time, her face flushes slightly. She has a sense of humour that remains unimpaired. "Yes," she will answer with a smile, "I am keeping very well, thank you. I am keeping my end up!"

— DR. ANTHONY CASPERS

By taking a piece of excised intestine and giving it a few clever twists,
Dr. Smörg could turn it into a poodle, giraffe, pony . . .

Getting Hosed

I remember an incident that occurred some years ago, which caused me acute embarrassment at the time, although I can laugh at it now.

Newly graduated from medicine, I was working in a small, rural Manitoba town and was keen to learn all the intricacies of managing a home, as well as my medical practice. With the bitter prairie winter approaching, a patient had advised me that it was a good idea to run the dryer vent into the basement instead of outside, so that all the nice, warm, humid air wouldn't be wasted. This seemed like a smart thing to do, so next Saturday morning found me perched on a ladder in the basement, working on the vent.

Something was needed to catch the lint, and my helpful patient advised me that the best screen was old panty hose, another logical suggestion. Just as I was reaching to put my wife's panty hose over the vent, the phone rang. It was the hospital. There was a "99" and I was on call for emergencies.

I hastily stuffed the panty hose into my back pocket and ran off to the hospital, which happened to be close by, across the back lane. During the rush, the panty hose slipped halfway out and was dangling in the breeze behind me.

Breathless and slightly dishevelled, I arrived in the resuscitation room and became engrossed in trying to stabilize the critically ill patient. After a while, several nurses began nudging one another and grinning at me. I was extremely annoyed. This wasn't a time for joking around; the patient's life was quickly ebbing away. A snicker broke out. Then another nurse peeked around the corner and winked at me!

Thoroughly upset now, I was just about to set these inconsiderate people straight when the head nurse sidled up to me, glanced at the dangling panty hose behind me, and said in a voice all could hear, "You son of a gun, you."

Well, the patient's face was deathly white while mine was crimson, with all facial arteries pulsating wildly, as the full meaning of her words hit me.

"You don't understand," I stammered, pulling out the incriminating panty hose. "This isn't mine. It's my wife's! I mean, it's her old panty hose!"

"Sure, sure," the nurse said. "I've heard all that before, but it's all right. This old fella's beyond hope, anyway, so why don't you go on home and finish what you were doing. I promise we won't call you for at least two hours."

It took me a long time to live that one down.

— DR. KLAUS DITTBERNER

I Left My Heart . . . to the Provincial Government

Every time I get a new issue of my driver's licence, I'm forced to do some uncomfortable soul-searching. As in most provinces, Ontario licences have a section that you fill in if you want to donate your body, or parts of it, for use in transplants or medical research in the event of your death. I'm ashamed to say it's always a difficult decision.

"Okay, for lunch you have a choice of liver, kidney, heart . . . oh, I'm sorry, this is your organ donor card."

I try to be coolheaded and objective about the subject. I'm certainly attuned to the medical and social issues involved, especially how ever-improving transplant technology is creating a need, often critical, for donor organs.

Not long ago a single organ transplant was a mind-boggling medical triumph, but today double and even triple transplants have become common. Some techno-prophets predict that soon we'll be able to replace all our major organs routinely as the need arises. ("Just change the liver and lungs, Doc, and while you got me open, get me an estimate on a new ticker, will ya?") We can only assume that in this Brave New World, newborn babies will come with standard factory warranties. So who am I to stand in the way of the march toward Utopia by selfishly clinging to my vital organs?

Still, I always hesitate before signing. Perhaps one reason is the provincial government logo at the top of the organ donor card. As soon as I see that the government's involved, I reread the form very carefully to make sure nobody's going to try to take any bodily parts from me before I'm dead. After all, the government's already taking an arm and a leg; who knows what they'll be asking for next?

Some of my mistrust probably stems from the heavy dose of science fiction I ingested as a teenager. I especially recall a society envisioned by writer Larry Niven, where the demand for organs was so great that all crimes, including repeat traffic offences, carried the death penalty — and subsequent disposal of the body to the state organ bank.

Of course, the real reason so many people choose not to donate their organs is because logic seldom wins out against those irrational fears and superstitions that we all harbour — especially when dealing with such weighty matters as death and the carving up of our corpses.

It's hardly surprising that many people like to pretend that the Grim Reaper will never find them. (Perhaps they'll be in the bathroom when he calls.) Signing an organ donor form amounts to an admission that they're going to die, so they simply throw it away and thus assure themselves of immortality.

There are others who don't donate their organs because they're not sure what happens after death and they want to hedge their bets. They figure it's prudent to hang on to everything they've got just in case they need it in the hereafter. (What a pity not to be able to see the others playing their harps and riding around on their clouds — and just because you gave away your eyeballs.)

Some people, like the ancient pharaohs, even ask to have their prize possessions buried with them . . . including cold hard cash. I can only presume that if they're right, they hope to have a shot at a McDonald's franchise in the afterworld.

Then there are those who not only refuse to volunteer any organs, but also have their bodies cryogenically preserved, in the belief that a future supercivilization will revive them and cure them of any terminal diseases they have. If they live in Ontario, my guess is that once they're resurrected, they'll have their bodies repossessed for back taxes owing and be sent off to the organ bank.

With so many people holding back their bodies and parts, the forces of economics have gone to work. In the United States the demand for some organs is so great that a black market has sprung up to provide a supply. There have been regular reports, for example, of poor, desperate people selling their kidneys for tens of thousands of dollars, and rumours persist of an organized murder ring that offers human organs for sale.

It may not be long before some people, instead of magnanimously donating their bodily parts to the public trust, start including them in their estates, to be disposed of in wills like other valuable property. ("To my wife, Mildred, who never stopped nagging me about my smoking and drinking, I leave my lungs and liver, and my stamp collection.")

But I'm proud to say that I've overcome my greed and superstitions and have signed my organ donor card. If, after I'm dead, I can alleviate another's suffering or save a life, then I'm proud to do it. Cut me up and pass me around. After death the body is just a useless, empty shell, and you can do with mine what you will! I'll be beyond caring.

Just keep my cadaver away from those medical students.

— DANNY DOWHAL

PART FOUR

Here and There

The Joy Of Obesity

Fat Is Where It's At

O **besity has been getting** a lot of bad press recently. Research, conducted entirely by thin people, has uncovered justification for their own masochistic, obsessive-compulsive, fun-killing, anal-retentive lifestyles.

One of the great problems with research, of course, is that the researchers tend to find what they're looking for. And when they find it they stop looking for other things. Also, research is often interpreted to match the views of the observer. It's important, therefore, not to believe research by any pressure group that starts with preconceived ideas.

Examples of findings not to believe: research on smoking by nonsmokers, on liver disease by nondrinkers, on the benefits of exercise by a physical education department, on the hazards of cholesterol by an anorexic, and on the joy of obesity by an overweight GP.

*"I was about to diagnose a severe
heart defect when I realized that my stethoscope
had picked up his personal stereo."*

"We're going to have to separate those two."

The whole obesity phobia was started by some statistics from a life insurance company purporting to show that people who were overweight didn't live as long as people who were underweight. These were very raw figures and led to some unwarranted conclusions.

First, it was assumed that if the overweight group lost weight they'd live longer. This was totally unproved. It never will be proved, as there are just not enough people to study who have lost weight permanently.

Second, it did not address the possibility that the obese group might have another factor affecting lifespan. It seems this is very likely, since the Framington Study showed that if diabetics and those with heart disease were removed from the obese group, the obese group then lived longer.

Let's list some benefits of obesity:

- Overeating is fun. Make a list of all the pleasures there are in this life, and you'll find the list isn't very long. The one pleasure that's lifelong and never pales is eating. It doesn't cause STDs, it can be done in public, and it's unlikely to lead to trouble with the college.
- Carrying fat is good exercise. If you believe in exercise (I don't), surely carrying around 20 or 30 pounds of fat all day should be good for you?

- Obese people are nicer people. This is not just a hasty remark, but the result of careful clinical observation. I've seen an average of 30 patients a day for 30 years, which comes to about 234,000 doctor/patient interactions. Stuff those figures in your computer and see the p factor.

I can tell you that obese people are more jolly, more kind, more forgiving, and just generally nicer. Although it could be the other way round: losing weight, and keeping it off, is so rare that only obsessive-compulsives are able to do it. This may be admirable, but obsessive-compulsives aren't relaxing people to be with.

- Obese people represent superior adaptation. In days gone by there were many advantages to being able to convert excess food into fat. The long winters were better survived by those with a reserve of calories.
- Climatic adaptation. Obese people can survive cold better. In particular, their cold-water survival superiority has been demonstrated many times.
- Obese people make better lovers. This is a fact known to romantics the world over. Bony lovers can never compete with what G. K. Chesterton referred to as the "promise of pneumatic bliss."
- Anorexia, a terrible condition, is rare among obese people.

"This randomized, double-blind trial involving over 20,000 patients was conducted over a 10 year period. Unfortunately we've forgotten why."

"Thank God I found you! I thought I was the only one —
I had no idea there were other smokers!"

Those who consider the highly trained athlete as the ideal human might want to consider the greatest duration runner of the animal kingdom, the pronghorn antelope of Wyoming. It can run at 95 kilometres per hour for an hour. It has tremendous lungs, an amazing cardiac output, and a maximum oxygen uptake that might deplete the Earth's resources. So why didn't this marvel of nature become a widespread species? Since these antelopes have no body fat and can stand neither cold nor lack of food, few survive the Wyoming winter.

Think about it.

— DR. JOHN COCKER

On Being a Doctor

"The art of medicine consists of amusing the patient while nature cures the disease."

— VOLTAIRE

"God heals and the doctor takes the fee."

— BENJAMIN FRANKLIN

"The oldest man alive today is reported to have celebrated his 139th birthday. His case is regarded as a triumph of nature over medical knowledge."

— OLIVER WENDELL HOLMES

"As long as men are liable to die and are desirous to live, a physician will be made fun of, but he will be well paid."

— LA BRUYÈRE

The GP's Nightmare

Don't tell the government about this, but we keep having this dream. Someone climbs up the water tower and puts cimetidine, ASA, amitriptyline, diazepam, and amoxicillin in the drinking water. The next day half the GPs in town have nothing to do.

The accommodation-arrangement charge is $20 per night, which includes a doctor's spouse.

— DOCTOR'S REVIEW

CTI Technologies Corporation believes it has found salvation in a condom it calls the Love Gasket. "One of the ideas was to put the word 'love' back into condoms," secretary-treasurer John Tomkins said. As for sales, "I think the main thrust is going into nontraditional areas."

— VANCOUVER SUN

New for the Nineties: Brand-name Diseases

From south of the border comes the disturbing news that the Funk and Wagnalls dictionary is considering adding Nintendo Neck to its lexicon of modern American-English terms. Nintendo Neck is an ailment afflicting some people, especially male preteens, who are fanatical players of home video games. These joystick junkies often play while lying on their bellies, and subsequently get a pain in the neck from looking up at their television screens. It's like a couch potato's version of tennis elbow.

The fact that today's passion for electronic games should have health repercussions is not what's disturbing, however. After all, we've safely established by now that virtually anything taken in sufficient megadoses can be bad for you. No, what's upsetting about the Nintendo Neck development is that it marks the entry of major corporations into the once-exclusive domain of doctors: naming diseases and medical conditions.

This could set medicine back a century! In the early days of modern medicine, of course, a doctor would literally make a name for himself by sticking it onto a new disease. No self-respecting household is ignorant of names such as Parkinson, Huntington, Hodgkin, and Alzheimer . . . just a few that spring immediately to mind.

Eventually the competition for naming diseases got so fierce that any patient appearing with a condition not instantly diagnosed was descended on by a deluge of doctors with a fortune-seeking fervour rivalled only by today's malpractice lawyers. Fortunately, as knowledge of human anatomy and biosystems expanded, the medical community grew more enlightened.

Diseases now took on long, compounded, exotic, scientific names like megahyperheteroviral stereonucleosis, streptotorycoccus, rubbertuberculosis, and amateurkaryotic. While doctors sacrificed individual fame by using this nomenclature for their new discoveries, the stature of the entire medical community was enhanced. Patients were comforted by the knowledge that a physician had to be an expert just to be able to pronounce such names, which made even the simplest medical disorder sound deadly serious.

Naturally competition among MDs conducting scientific research has remained intense, not so much in order to have their names attached to fashionable new diseases but rather to ensure they get a healthy portion of the grant money that's provided by governments and institutions. Today, though, much of that money is administered by laymen and politicians,

"So much for your miracle cure for hemorrhoids!"

so the naming of new disorders must follow some of the rules of advertising and marketing. The names should have pizzazz and be easy to remember, yet still keep that reassuring scientific flavour.

First came the practice of using abbreviations in place of lengthy words or phrases — TB, MS, CF. A more recent refinement has been to string together words whose initials then form a punchy acronym, preferably one that can itself be pronounced as a monosyllable. To date, the highest achievement of this minor art has been AIDS, one of the media darlings of the eighties and nineties, whose surrounding publicity has translated into big bucks in terms of research funding.

Not surprisingly, many labs are hiring PR firms to help give their diseases a high profile. Rumour has it that a Toronto marketing outfit has already coined the hot new Canadian illness of the nineties — something nasty called GST.

Which brings us back to the frightening precedent that's being set by Nintendo and its Neck. If this idea takes hold, it won't be long before the big multinationals, with their experience in product promotion and their well-established corporate identities, will corner the market on diseases. Soon they'll be adding lucrative research grants to their marketing budgets. Before we know it the media will be dominated by stories about Apple Eye (from staring too long at computer screens), Bombardier Bottom (a hemorrhoidal condition peculiar to snowmobilers), and Campeau Cramp (from trying to swallow too much). Corporate raiders will launch takeover bids to gain other companies' disease portfolios. By the year 2000 business school grads will have to be MDs as well as MBAs if they want to be on the fast track.

Talk about your pain in the neck!

— DANNY DOWHAL

Three-month suspended sentences handed to 102 anti-abortionists in Vancouver are "a miscarriage of justice," the vice president of the local Pro-Life Society said on Monday.

— KAMLOOPS DAILY NEWS

"Dyslexics are normal people. It is not a disease. We do not criticize people for being colour blind. Why can't people just accept dyslecixs?" he asked.

— LANCASTER GUARDIAN

"I wish you'd called me sooner, Mrs. Moodie."

Technostress

A Nuisance Whose Time Has Come

The stress of adapting to the age of high technology is widely believed to befall only those who work with computers on their desks. Nothing could be further from the truth. Technology affects us all, even if indirectly, every day.

Examples abound of the ordinary sort of household appliances that are prone to stress-inducing malfunctions, but the problem knows no class boundaries. Even the wealthy are not immune.

Let's look in on the morning activities of one of the elite. Charles is chairman of the board, and his daily routine reflects his high personal standards of excellence.

He is awakened this morning, as is his custom, at 6:02 a.m. Stepping into his exercise outfit (which has, of course, been laid out for him), he does his 55-minute weight-lifting and aerobics workout, finishing with a whirlpool and shower. He's then served a spa breakfast, containing precisely 600 calories, on china and linen at the pool terrace.

Ten minutes later, after slipping into his worsted Savile Row suit, he retires to his library desk for an hour's orderly review of his financial empire in preparation for this morning's annual board meeting. Ah, how nice to be in total control of one's life!

Suddenly technostress leaps out in ambush! One of the burglar-proof gold locks on Charles's designer briefcase has jammed shut, with both keys inside. The batteries of his new microdictation machine have gone flat because he inadvertently left it running during yesterday's lunch. His $3,000 limited edition platinum fountain pen (a gift from his third wife) has just snapped its snorkel and dribbled ink all over the Louis XIV desktop. The $1,200 matching pencil has run out of lead. In the top drawer are 17 different sizes of lead refills, but extensive experimentation reveals that none of them fits the pencil.

Infuriated, Charles decides to set off for the office. He approaches his stable of fine motor cars, takes the new microwave remote-control garage door opener out of his jacket pocket, and presses the button. All of his garage doors remain closed, but his neighbour's opened.

Finally managing to pry open one of his doors with a spade, Charles turns his attention to the cars. The Mercedes won't start because the battery is dead: the local mechanic shorted the electric seat warmers. He can't even get into his new Lincoln, since he's lost the combination to the space-age push-button door locks. The Ferrari hasn't gone anywhere for six weeks, pending the arrival of spare parts from Milan. The Jaguar is in the shop once again, being fitted with the only accessory that didn't come standard, namely a trailer hitch on the front.

Now late for his board meeting, Charles considers his options and heads for the staff quarters for help. He finally arrives for the meeting with face florid and ulcer nearing, an enraged and technostressed passenger in his gardener's flatbed petunia truck.

If any of this sounds familiar to you, then consider my two rules for combatting technostress:

Rule No. 1: Before you buy even one more gadget, ask yourself, "Do I really need this?" Chances are you don't.

Rule No. 2: If you do really need this, then for heaven's sake keep the instructions. You may think you're blessed with superb powers of deductive and inductive reasoning, but then why is it that you can't get your VCR to blink anything except "12:00 SUN"? Keep a file just for instruction booklets for all your gadgets and your life will be at least a little less stressful in this technological age.

— DR. PETER HANSON

Price And Value

I often tell my clients who want to know how much I get paid for a house call that I get almost as much as the Maytag repairman. Back in 1969 or so, when I was a young doctor and just before medicare came to the Province of Quebec, I made many house calls, and very often during weekends. One Sunday morning I went to see a guy who had a pulmonary infection. I examined him and gave him an IM shot of antibiotics.

He was still lying in bed when his wife asked me how much she owed me. I told her that my fee, including the needle, was $10. She reacted very strongly to this, telling me that I was very expensive, et cetera.

I asked her if she'd ever called a plumber on a Sunday for a house call, so she could compare that cost with mine. The guy started laughing and told his wife to pay me and stop arguing. Then he looked at me and said, "I'm a plumber and I never do house calls on weekends."

— DR. GUY LANDRY

[Soccer club] **Oxford United have lost out on the chance to have the safest defence in the land. Condom firm Mates was asked to consider a sponsorship deal with the club — but pulled out before negotiations reached a climax.**

— OXFORD COURIER

"You've got us bafffled, Mr. Messiter. The strings of your heart do go zing, but we can't seem to find out why."

My Career as a Drug Runner

t's difficult for anyone going on holiday to decide what medical items to take. It's even more difficult for a physician, since the possible choice is larger. Should you take just a few aspirins and some Band-Aids? Or go to the other extreme and pack a boxful of old samples?

Some years ago my wife, Monica, and I sailed across the Atlantic, and I faced the task of selecting emergency first-aid equipment. I started out with scissors, forceps, and needle holder. But then things began to escalate. Suture material, catgut, retractors?

What type of surgery might be involved? We would be at sea for a maximum of four weeks, but during that time there could be no outside assistance. After the first two days, we'd certainly be out of reach of helicopters.

I tried to think of likely medical disasters that might befall us. Burns were very possible, since we cooked with propane and had a gasoline generator. Sterile burn dressings are expensive and would be hard to store, so I opted for extra rolls of Saran Wrap to use for dressings — it might be sterile.

Appendicitis? With my rusty surgical skills this would best be best treated with antibiotics and parenteral fluids. IV fluids are hard to carry, but rectal fluids would be something we could manage.

Strangulated hernia? A famous doctor/sailor, Dr. Pye of Moonraker, died at sea from this very problem after sailing many thousands of miles. I had no idea what we'd have done under similar circumstances — some kind of surgery to open the hernial orifice, maybe.

150

"I've only got herpes!"

Fractures? I carried a complete set of inflatable splints, which are ideal on small boats. They take up very little room, work well for immobilization, and act as padding for comfort.

Drugs were a special problem. I took analgesics, antibiotics, antihistamines, Tagamet, and a lot of out-of-date samples. For injectables, the most important was morphine. But how much to take?

We could be at sea for, say, four weeks with severe burns or a compound fracture, so if the morphine was q6h, we could need about 80 ampoules. This was where the problem began, as we were going to many different countries, some of which might have rigid ideas about visitors carrying 80 ampoules of morphine.

Not declaring drugs for customs seemed to be less trouble than declaring them, so I packed all the injectables separately, labelled them SHIP'S STORES, and then locked them up. This seemed reasonable to me, and I just hoped that any customs person might also see it as reasonable.

As it happened, no one ever even asked what drugs we carried. We visited more than 30 countries, and the subject never came up. Instead we were grilled about firearms and electronic equipment, and I was asked about being a physician.

I carried the narcotics halfway round the world and never had a problem until we decided to sell the boat in Turkey. Many North Americans' ideas about travelling in Turkey come from the movie *Midnight Express*. In fact, that was nowhere near the truth. The customs officers were fierce, but the people we met were charming.

However, it took a day to clear us and our vessel through customs, including a visit to the port doctor. For this visit I had to walk across the town, explain to a bored receptionist why I'd come, fill out a form, and then sit outside the doctor's office for an hour.

The doctor kept me waiting for an hour, during which I could see him through the office window sitting with his feet up,

"Let's see now . . . 'ribbed' . . . 'lubricated' . . . 'extra-thin' . . .
nope, sorry, no thermal."

reading. This was usual in the Mediterranean: people of inferior rank are kept waiting to remind them of their subservient position in life. I've often wondered if some of my colleagues keep patients waiting for the same reason.

When the port doctor called me in, he stamped our papers without looking at them and waved me away. I didn't embarrass him by letting him know I was a fellow physician.

We sold our boat in Turkey for an offer we couldn't refuse. I came back to Canada to start work again, and Monica stayed to complete the paperwork. An early problem she faced was what to do with the morphine. The boat purchaser wasn't a physician and wouldn't want to carry narcotics. But how to get rid of it?

The whole port area was guarded by the Turkish police — in fact, the entire country was a police state. (Some Turkish physician friends said they preferred the police state. When there was a democracy, the streets weren't safe.)

Monica decided to dispose of the morphine surreptitiously. She broke each ampoule and shook it so that the contents went down the sink. Next came the problem of getting rid of the ampoules, which had MORPHINE written across them in large red letters. The garbage might be searched, but the harbour had deep water and was polluted, like all Mediterranean harbours. She opted to flush the glass ampoules down the head.

Things were fine until she got in the dinghy to go ashore. There, to her horror, were all the glass ampoules, floating round the boat, clearly marked MORPHINE. Some were stuck to the side of the hull. So, with an oar, she started to hit them against the hull to try to crush them. This made quite a commotion.

It was at this point that she looked up and saw a Turkish policeman watching her from the dock. He looked straight at her and then beckoned her toward him.

Monica climbed up onto the dock and stood before him. The thought of 20 years in a Turkish prison crossed her mind. The policeman glowered. His hand rested lightly on his machine gun.

"Your flag," he hissed. "She is torn. A disgrace to the Turkish people."

"All those in favour, say eye . . ."

I should explain that a yacht carries on the stern the flag of the country where it is registered. At the starboard yardarm the flag of the country being visited is flown as a "courtesy flag." Our Turkish flag, of very poor quality, had been flying for several months.

Monica started to breathe again. "I'm sorry," she said. "I'll get a new one tomorrow."

"A disgrace to the country!" He repeated. "My brother, he sells very good flags. Here is his card."

The next day Monica bought the best flag in the store, and several other items from the brother. The rest of the ampoule evidence was recovered, crushed, and sent to the bottom of the harbour, where it remains to this day.

The weather was cool when Monica completed the sale of the boat and, with some relief, left the country. She later referred to this event as quitting cold Turkey.

— DR. JOHN COCKER

The erect penis of a blue whale may be eight or ten feet long. Early whalers used to cut around the organ at the base, strip off the skin and use it in the manufacturing of customized golf bags. According to one authority, the golf bag from the Blue Whale is creamy white flecked with irregular stripes of blue-grey, while that from a Fin is creamy white without any flecks. Presumably, the genitals of other species are too small to hold a regulation size golf club.

— THE ROUNDER, NEWFOUNDLAND AND LABRADOR RURAL DEVELOPMENT COUNCIL

Administratium
A Breakthrough in Atomic Physics Has Elemental Implications for Doctors

Thanks to our colleagues in atomic physics, we are able to announce the discovery of a new and hitherto undreamed-of element, and also its linkage — which may be causal — to a certain common but poorly understood disease of physicians.

The description of Administratium (Ad), the heaviest element known, stems from original observations made in the office of the president of one of our great universities while it was being swept for bugs. A completely new type of interference prevented any meaningful readings by the most sensitive instruments, and this was finally traced to massive concentration of this previously undescribed element. Its virtual immunity to scientific detection is due to its enormous atomic mass and almost total inertia — total to the physicist, although as we shall see, it's far from inert medically.

The Administratium atom is composed of one neutron, 125 assistants to the neutron, 75 vice-neutrons, and 111 assistants to the vice-neutrons, for an atomic mass of 312. The outer shell, which one would expect to be occupied by electrons, is usually empty, although high concentrations may attract an orbiting ring of elegant secretaries and nubile personal assistants. The nucleus is held together by exchange of mesonlike particles, termed "memos."

Being devoid of electrons, Administratium is inert, and also has the property of impeding reactions by normally active particles. A very small concentration will lengthen reaction times interminably, from a few seconds to several days or weeks; in extreme cases the reaction may come to a halt or even reverse. This has been noted in the offices of Deans.

Another feature of its inertia is a process inverse to that of radioactive decay, by which the element increases in quantity over a period of time. This may be cyclic, in a manner analogous to DNA synthesis. The biological analogies are intriguing, and we shall return to them later.

Administratium does display some properties resembling magnetism. It's repelled by the type of activity found in hospitals, especially in ORs, ICUs, and Emergency Departments, and it will achieve its greatest concentration as remotely as possible from these. In one hospital, where the ICU and OR are in the basement, this effect has reached antigravitational force, and Administratium is detected most commonly on the topmost floor of the building. In another, neighbouring institution, it's only found in a separate building.

Administratium occurs in very marked form in the Business Class areas of jet aircraft. In addition, it has an affinity or attraction for large mahogany desks, thick carpets, and chairs with very high backs. It may even be generated in such locations, just as grey fluff is under beds.

Of most interest to medicine are the toxic effects of Administratium. One symptom of exposure, sometimes even in low concentrations, is massive depression and inertia, presumably related to the element's heaviness. For this reason certain areas where Administratium appears in almost pure form are termed "Bored Rooms."

However, a paradoxical finding in those who receive huge doses of Administratium may be a form of addiction, as to a narcotic drug, and tolerance is evinced by random, purposeless, self-serving activity distinguished by total irrelevance to any external, objective criteria. Delusions of achievement with compulsive self-congratulation are frequent, and may be mutual in a group of sufferers.

Another variant, similar to a form of organic mental disease, is compulsive auto-omphaloscopy with voluminous recording of observations. This has been noted most commonly in accreditation systems.

This strange element may, by its size and complexity, be approaching a "life-form" similar to a prion, and achieving the capacity for self-replication. In the health-care professions frequent exposure leads to immunity, or to sensitization with violent rejection reactions provoked by even a trace of the substance. However, if the immune system is compromised in some way not fully understood, possibly by exhaustion, a type of infection can occur, and an apparently normal physician can become a focus for replication and dissemination. It has been suggested by some that this may be a voluntary process, and the patient's own "fault," but others believe it to be due to an inborn or genetic error of mental metabolism, for which there is no cure.

There are analogies to alcoholism. The patient totally lacks insight and will vehemently deny that anything is wrong. Frequently the physical characteristics of the element are transferred to the infected person, who experiences irresistible repulsion from normal medical activity and will most likely come to reside as near to the Bored Room as possible; in extreme cases this will be permanent.

In these unfortunates, physical appearance is normally impaired, but even a few moments' conversation will lead the acute clinician to diagnosis of this most distressing disease. There is no effective therapy, and no hope of cure; the disease is commonly progressive. Strong doses of humour may be protective, but avoidance of exposure, as in rabies, is the best prophylactic.

— DR. HARRY EMSON

The Evolution of a Biker

I think it was Shakespeare who said that in one life a man plays many roles. In my experience that goes double for a woman, particularly if that woman rides a motorcycle.

It all started in 1969 when I was putting myself through university. An archetypal Impecunious Student, I had $800 and no vehicle.

Eight hundred dollars would buy me an old car, cheap to insure, expensive to fix. Eight hundred dollars would also buy me a small, new motorcycle, cheap to run and to fix. "Aha," I said to myself, "a motorcycle will be just the thing." Of course, I'd never actually driven anything with a motor, let alone a motorcycle.

I consulted a friend of mine who was the proud owner of a Honda 100. She offered to let me try it. With great faith she started the bike and demonstrated the controls. I slid on and shot triumphantly up the alley. On my return I forgot how to brake, so I improvised by shifting down and tipping into the ditch. The bike and I rose out of the ditch, the bike wreathed in leaves, and I in smiles.

My friend was dubious about my prognosis as a biker, but it was too late. I'd been transformed into a Biker to Be. I promptly purchased a brand-new Honda 100 of my own, thus establishing myself as a Beginning Biker (var. Incompeta). Every day I practised riding the poor thing. I stalled it and I flooded it and I dropped it and I popped inadvertent wheelies.

One day the bike stopped and wouldn't start, probably in self-defence. Unable to diagnose the problem, I phoned the bike salesman in desperation. "I don't know what's wrong," I wailed.

He very kindly came by, trying hard not to smile, and poured some gas into the tank. Sure enough . . .

Things picked up after that, and I graduated into a Basic Biker (var. Utilitaria). I rode through rain, sun, sleet, glare ice, snow, and hail, developing a fine scorn for what I called Sunshine Bikers. On one particularly snowy day, my bike was the only wheeled vehicle to make it up the mountain to Simon Fraser University — with 10 fellow students all pushing!

The main hazard, however, wasn't weather but car drivers. It seemed that they either couldn't see me or didn't like me. Worst were those who purposely forced me off the road, or got in front of me, then threw open all four doors and slammed on the brakes.

One notable exception to this hostility occurred on a sunny day when I suddenly had to go somewhere while my jeans were in the wash. Against my better judgement, for I am very fond of my dermis, I rode off wearing a skirt. I soon found myself escorted by a coterie of convertibles and muscle cars driven by cheering young men. It was lovely. It was also, alas, my only experience of Biker as Sex Symbol.

It's well-known that Vancouver weather is more often rain than sun — I was soon saving for a set of Belstaff rain gear. I invested in the best gum boots to be found in the Army and Navy Boutique, and sewed vinyl hand protectors for my handlebars. I also acquired a top box to hold my books and supplies, and a little windshield. I began to feel quite well equipped — the Biker Compleat, if you will.

It was then that the Harley Biker of Simon Fraser took me in hand. He was a huge, gentle man with an enormous black beard. He usually parked his Harley close to my Honda.

One day he spoke to me. "Cute little scooter," he said, indicating my bike. "You should chain her up."

"Nobody could steal her. I always lock the forks," I replied.

The Harley Biker's lips twitched. He leaned over, effortlessly picked up my motorcycle with one hand, and tucked it under his arm. "Where would you like me to put her?" he inquired.

"I'll get a chain tonight," I said.

The chain presented a new problem: where should it go when I was riding the bike? I didn't want it on the top box getting my books all dirty, or around the bike frame scratching the paint. Finally I settled on wrapping it around my waist.

I was thus attired — in black Belstaff gear and gum boots, with my helmet on, my faceplate steamed up and my chain wrapped around my waist — that I stopped at a busy 24-hour grocery late one rainy night.

"I want you to meet Miss Hepworth — she's also on anticoagulants and diuretics."

I suddenly noticed that whatever aisle I entered was quickly vacated by the other shoppers. I couldn't figure it out. Then I took off my helmet and shook out my long hair, transforming myself from Brutish Biker to mild-mannered Girl in Rain Gear. The other shoppers gradually reappeared. Some of them even smiled at me.

The years passed and I entered medical school. Of course, I travelled to classes, as always, in jeans, helmet, and rain gear. Then, in second year, I went to the Medical Ball. My escort picked me up in his nice, warm, dry car. My hair was loose, and I was wearing makeup and a slinky floor-length gown.

As the evening progressed, two of my classmates, looking puzzled, studied me for a long time. Finally they pulled my escort aside. "Hey," they asked him, "who's the chick?" Obviously they couldn't connect the Femme Fatale with the Biker Compleat.

Nowadays, of course, I usually drive a car. But sometimes, on sunny days, when a bike's handy, I take the bike. The wind rush and road feel come back all over again, but somehow it's not quite the same.

It seems that I've turned into a Sunshine Biker!

— DR. GILLIAN ARSENAULT

"At parties, Melvyn, why do you insist on labelling everyone?"

Risks, You Say?

"**I**f the defendant had known** that this medication carried risks, he would not have taken it." Presumably he would not have driven to the court, taken the elevator, eaten his breakfast, or even gotten up in the morning. Where do patients and courts get the idea that one of our options in life is to be risk-free?

It seems to me that what we need is a unit of risk. Then doctors can tell their patients what will be acceptably "safe" for them. If they drive a car, for instance, they're prepared to accept a certain degree of risk. If they ride a motorbike, it gives a different message, and a different unit of risk.

This would help to rationalize our activity, and our advice to patients. It might also help prevent anomalies, such as the patient who smokes, but drinks bottled water because tap water might contain impurities.

Professor Trevor Kletz of Loughborough University in England has studied risk and has proposed a unit of risk based on smoking 100 cigarettes. The following activities involve a risk equivalent to that of smoking 100 cigarettes:

"First the good news. His temperature has gone down."

- Driving a car 4,000 miles.
- Working in the chemical industry for one year.
- Driving a motorbike for 350 hours.
- Drinking 40 bottles of wine.
- Eating 80 jars of peanut butter.
- Working in the home for two years (16 hours a day).
- Rock climbing for two hours.
- White-water canoeing for two hours.

Home appears to be one of the most hazardous places around. In Britain 500 children a year are killed accidentally in the home. But it won't help to step outside — 27 people a year are killed by automatic garage doors in the United States.

Maybe we should leave the city and step into the countryside, where every year bees and wasps kill one person in every 10 million. On the other hand, what about all those things that are known to be highly risky — for example, how about the toxins in the atmosphere and our water supply? Every environmentalist will tell you of the hazards of pollution.

But how many deaths per annum can really be attributed to dioxin, or to PCBs? It's in the region of zero. Compare that to the thousands of deaths annually that are a direct result of smoking, or car accidents.

Then there's nuclear power — widely feared because it's so widely misunderstood. However, we can't measure its hazards against an absolute zero, so we have to compare it with the alternatives. Consider that 27,000 people have died in coal-mining accidents in this century. The number killed in all nuclear power accidents, including Chernobyl, is a tiny fraction of that.

These are all factors to keep in mind when a smoker tells you he doesn't "believe in drugs," or when a rock climber tells you he doesn't want an IVP.

Back to the first paragraph. If it's not safe to get up in the morning, it surely must be safe to stay in bed. But the unfortunate fact is that more people die in bed than anywhere else.

— DR. JOHN COCKER

"Is there a second opinion in the house?"

The Incredible Shrinking Tour

Theme tours are highly popular these days. If we're so inclined, we can choose from cruises for singles, bus trips to visit the home of Elvis, or flights to historical sites in the Andes. But one popular theme that has been overlooked — until now — is what might be titled Travel for the Terrific, or Jaunts for Giants, or Expeditions for the Expansive, or Vacations for the Vast, or (let's not be too coy about it), Fun for Fatties.

Your body knows no limits — why should your travels?

Millions are made from the guilt that has been loaded on those of us who are lipidinously challenged. Join us as we cash in on treating this untreatable condition.

Our weight-loss tour will begin with a flight to Mexico City. I suggest splurging a bit and going Business Class. There's no point in starting a serious diet on an empty stomach. Eat all you can, but I would avoid food with sharp edges: these may hurt during what we'll call the rejection phase.

Once in Mexico City, we'll begin the program by eating a large bowl of unwashed salad. These greens are locally grown, with no artificial fertilizer. In fact, the fertilizer they use is so natural that the smell can still be detected. Better than a lot of unnatural chemicals.

The changes that result from the introduction of new intestinal flora and fauna (watch those fauna go!) is one of the most natural ways of losing weight rapidly — and I mean rapidly. This weight loss is readily discernible to the eyes, and to the nose.

(You'll appreciate now the earlier remark about avoiding food with sharp corners. To paraphrase Galileo, what goes down must come up. Or was it Newton?)

Recovering somewhat from the diet of salad, you'll be amazed by how much your appetite has already decreased. In fact, the very mention of food will cause waves of further potential weight loss, so keep a basin handy.

Next, all aboard for our flight to Egypt. Don't bother with Business Class this time. In Cairo we'll head down the main avenue, past the Kentucky Fried Chicken Palace, to a small wheelbarrow on a side street, where we'll all enjoy the locally made ice cream. It's even made from local water — from the picturesque canal that serves so many purposes for the neighbourhood where it's made. The water isn't artificially stabilized through all those processes that remove so much of the flavour from the waters of North America.

After a few days in the local hospital, where polio is much more than just another vaccine, we're ready for the next part of our vacation: the Mediterranean cruise. The cruise ship, specially designed for our program, has the new "reverse-action stabilizers." Instead of removing the pleasant roll of the ship, they accentuate it, so the ship lies first on one side and then the other. This rhythmic progress is so conducive to weight loss that even the crew members look like out-patients at the anorexia nervosa clinic.

You'll be helped ashore when we arrive at our scenic destination: Palermo, Sicily, home of the Mafia. Here we'll visit the underground catacombs where you may see the partially preserved corpses of previous citizens, still in their rotting clothing, all hanging from hooks in the wall. This will have such an effect on any remaining appetite that the next part of your holiday, the flight home, will come as a welcome relief.

We guarantee that you'll really look forward to your return to work (as soon as the Health Department has cleared you), and you'll delight in showing off your new, thinner self to your admiring colleagues.

— DR. JOHN COCKER

Fast Lane to a Longer Life?

Someone once asked Woody Allen if he wanted to achieve immortality through his films. "No," he replied, "I want to achieve immortality through not dying."

And so do we all. Most of us, anyway. Or at least we want to postpone the inevitable, live in good health to a ripe old age, and die after a brief illness. We call it minimizing risk factors.

Today the most fashionable risk factor is still cholesterol; science has clearly shown that if you reduce your serum cholesterol, you can die of homicide instead of a heart attack. Therefore, healthy octogenarians inquire about their cholesterol status and middle-aged sedentary smokers who wouldn't follow a diet to win a bet will pay homage to health by getting their cholesterol checked.

I suppose I'm a little cynical about cholesterol. Deep in my heart I'm convinced that in the next cycle we'll discover that we've been measuring the wrong thing, and that milk and eggs are good for you, after all. Meanwhile, I do feel obliged to follow contemporary practice and treat high-serum cholesterol levels in my patients, but I always wonder in the back of my mind if I'm really doing them any good.

Other roads to longevity warrant exploration. A few years ago I attended a Continuing Medical Education session on geriatrics. A cell biologist gave an intriguing talk on longevity, complete with graphs, based on experiments on rats and cats.

Female animals live longer than males. Well we know that. So I've picked the right sex for longevity. And males live longer if they're castrated. (We'll skip over this in terms of practical application in humans.) But here's the novel part: animals live nearly 50 percent longer if they're fed every second day instead of every day!

I was fascinated. Is regular fasting the road to longevity in humans? If I fast every other day, will I live to 120? What about two days a week? Fired with enthusiasm, I decided to give it a try.

I hadn't actually fasted since I lost my faith in my early twenties; back then I assumed it was the water deprivation that accounted for the headache and lassitude that accompanied a 24-hour fast. So the day after the CME conference I drank water and ate no food and went about my usual weekend chores.

But a weekend day was a bad choice. By the time I'd taken the bread out of the oven at half past three, my fast was abandoned. I decided to give it another try on Wednesday; that was the day I was always in a rush and didn't have time to eat, anyway — ideal for a fast.

I got up in the morning, had a glass of water, and went to the office. At noon I went on rounds, then had a glass of water and went back to work. So far so good.

But all afternoon I was irritable and uncomfortable and had difficulty concentrating. It didn't go well at all. Evening came and I served my husband and children their supper, then went into another room.

When I awoke the next morning, I wasn't even hungry; I just felt rotten. I ate a dish of yogurt and jam, and in about half an hour I was my normal, cheerful self again.

After that I gave up fasting as a route to longevity. Maybe it works and maybe it doesn't, but I decided it wasn't worth it. A short life but a merry one.

— DR. JEANNIE ROSENBERG

A Spleen-breaking Tale

It seems strange that while there are organizations to protect, defend, and promote your heart, your lungs, your kidneys, and almost every other organ, there isn't one fund-raiser who cares a whit about the most marvellous organ of all, the spirited spleen — that seat of mirth, courage, and anger.

Certainly long overdue is the founding of a World Spleen Association. With an initial annual budget of $3 million or so, the association would plan an all-out effort to make the world more knowledgeable, more conscious, and more concerned about who knows how many millions of spleens.

Basically the spleen has an image problem. Look at the heart, for example. People have come to believe the heart is the centre of love, intuition, and all that's good and sweet in the human spirit. But what is the heart? Just a big, fat muscle that lies around in your chest expanding and contracting.

"Just a minor complication, darling. He swallowed the spoon."

What's the heart got that the spleen doesn't have? A good public relations campaign, that's all.

The association's immediate goal would be to stamp out the centuries-old discrimination against the spleen. There's absolutely no logical reason that the spleen cannot perform exactly the same literary functions as the heart, as a reading of a model short story will demonstrate. Here's how the text of such a story would read.

Coleslaw Wabels was a stout-spleened country boy from the spleenland of Canada, alone for the first time in the big city — until he met Sweetbread Monroe, a singer with a spleen of gold whose favourites were the popular "Spleen and Soul," "My Spleen Belongs to Daddy," "Deep in the Spleen of Texas," and "Peg o' My Spleen."

Innocent Coleslaw lost his spleen to Sweetbread on the spot. "Please," he pleaded, "let's have a spleen-to-spleen talk. I hope you won't think I wear my spleen on my sleeve, but you've captured my spleen. It's yours."

Sweetbread, who had a spleen as big as all outdoors, was touched.

"To get to the spleen of the matter," she confided, "I've always yearned in the secret recesses of my spleen for a soft-spleened man like you. Let our spleens be eternally intertwined."

Coleslaw's spleen leaped. "My spleen is too full to talk," he whispered.

And in the weeks that followed he plied her with spleen-shaped boxes of candy, drawings of spleens pierced by arrows, and reams of spleensick poetry.

But it was not to be.

"Coleslaw," Sweetbread said sadly one day, "I know this will cause you much spleenache, but I've had a change of spleen. Another swain has stolen my spleen away."

Coleslaw's spleen sank. He placed his hand over his belly. "Cross my spleen, but you're a cold-spleened wench," he cried, "for you have broken my spleen!" With that he collapsed of a spleen attack. He was saved only by a miraculous spleen transplant operation.

Sweetbread went on to a brilliant career. The whole nation took her to its spleen, and she became known as "Canada's Sweetspleen." Ironically she never knew that the theme song

"Okay, Doctor, I'll take two aspirins and call you in the morning, but I don't see how that will put out your chimney fire."

that sparked her success had been written by the spleen-broken Coleslaw after his transplant operation. It was called "I Left My Spleen in San Francisco."

— JOHN KEEFAUVER

House Calls in the Country

I wasn't in practice in Saskatchewan very long before I learned to treat any house call with the greatest suspicion if told, "You can't miss it."

"You go three miles past the little wooden bridge and then turn right" was a set of directions I particularly remember, as it turned out that the bridge had been replaced by a culvert a few years earlier.

"The road is fine. You won't have any trouble" was also to be taken with a large grain of salt. After I was given one such assurance, I drove my poor car through mudhole after mudhole until I came across a farmer trying to drain off one of the more impressive ponds on the road. When I asked how the road was up ahead, on the way to old Joe's, he said, "Nothing has been able to get over it for the past two weeks. But the same goes for the road you just came over."

Thus encouraged, I skidded my way to Joe's, who admitted he hadn't been off the farm for a few weeks — "but the road was fine then."

Country calls could be a real trial in the spring, summer, and fall, but in the winter they could be positively dangerous. There was a lethal potential, in the middle of the night when it was minus 20 degrees F or colder, in getting stuck and having to walk.

When the drifts on the road grew too high for the plows to handle, a detour would be made across the fields, and when that drifted over, they'd make a detour from the detour! So in a storm, with everything drifting in, you had to choose the most recently opened route. If you chose wrong, you had to dig yourself out and try another.

The longer I practised, and the more close shaves I had, the more I insisted that someone come partway to meet me. I also tried to take someone along with me — for the first few years my long-suffering wife.

Once, after getting stuck in a drift, I walked for an hour and got frozen cheeks in the process. As I walked into the farmyard, I heard the tractor being started up, as had been promised. When I asked the farmer why he'd waited so long, he replied, "I had to have breakfast, you know."

On yet another occasion, after a week of heavy winds, with virtually all the side roads blocked by drifts, I was talked into making a night call by the promise that a truckload of men would come to meet me on Highway 1 and bring me to the farm.

I was very short of sleep and had a heavy day coming up, so I became increasingly impatient as I waited in my car from 11:30 to 12:30 with no sign of the truck. Eventually I decided to go as far as I could, and the truck and men could get my car free.

The drifts had piled up so much that there was seldom a sign of the road but, amazingly, the snow had been packed so hard by the wind that I could drive over it. I expected to break through at any time, going up and over some of the big drifts, so I was driving very gently, if you know what I mean. However, my luck held and I reached the farm, where everyone was puzzled by the lack of truck and men.

It turned out that the road I'd come over had been abandoned weeks before, and the truck was following a field trail opened by a bulldozer. I finished my work and drove back to the highway with similar luck, taking the abandoned road once more, against advice.

I later found that the poor guys in the truck had been thoroughly stuck and didn't get through to the highway until morning — "and Doc wasn't there!"

So it is, with country calls as it is with life, "better to be lucky than good."

— DR. BRADLEY HOUSTON

"And for the upwardly mobile doctor,
our deluxe Model 2000
medical bag has a built-in cellular phone
plus a food synthesizer
that produces real hospital food."

Always Expect the Unexpected

It's touching how laypeople trust their physicians to know about other creatures. Thus, a neighbour, in an "over-the-fence" consultation, asked me about the strange behaviour pattern of her dog. This collie, formerly of sound mind, had taken to putting his head in the fireplace, looking up, and barking.

We discussed schizophrenia, paranoia, neuroses, and isn't it amazing how animals seem to get the same ills that humans do? As the dog didn't have an OHIP number, my interest began to wane.

Anyway, before I had time to come up with a definitive diagnosis, the neighbour made her own. She'd noted a raccoon sitting on the top of the chimney.

Now the problem was more simple: how to get rid of the raccoon. She tried lighting a fire, which worked at first. Then she called in the animal control people, who put wire over the chimney top and a raccoon-repelling substance on the brickwork. Each of these techniques seemed to work for a short time, but now there were two raccoons living in the chimney, and from experience we knew that where there are two raccoons, more will surely follow.

The neighbour then heard of some local folklore. If a radio playing raucous rock and roll, reggae, heavy metal, or other children's music were put in the fireplace, facing up the chimney, the raccoons would go.

So an old radio was placed in the fireplace, music blasted forth and, lo and behold, it worked. The raccoons packed up all their belongings and moved off, never to be seen there again.

That should be the end of the story, but a few weeks later I was stopped by a neighbour who lived farther down the street: "I wonder if I could talk to you about our dog. She's been behaving very strangely lately. . ."

When I went straight from internship into compulsory military service, I got a crash course on how to deal with bureaucracy. This training has become more valuable now as government interference in medical care increases almost daily.

A more senior medical officer gave me lots of advice, such as: "Always deal with more than one topic per letter. The bureaucrat can only think of one thing at a time."

Another useful hint was: "If there's something you really want, and you apply for it, it's likely to be turned down because bureaucrats are always working under 'fiscal restraint.'" The technique here is to ask for something outrageous that you don't really want, and then, as an afterthought, ask for what you do really want. This is based on the theory that saying no requires some emotional energy, and once this energy is spent there's none left to resist the next request. Teenage children know this empirically, and can switch from "Can I have a TV in my room?" to "Well, can I borrow the car then?" just like professional negotiators.

In the small military hospital where I worked we had a problem. The X-ray room had a door that was too narrow. We met situations where an injured soldier on a stretcher would be carried to the door, would have to get off the stretcher, stand while the stretcher was manoeuvred through the door, and then climb back onto the stretcher. I applied to have the door widened, but with no result.

Using my newly acquired technique to confuse the bureaucrats, I then applied for a completely new X-ray building, giving only a few halfhearted reasons why this was essential. In a final paragraph I suggested that if a new room wasn't possible, could the door be widened?

"There's nothing much I can do. It's a slipped disc."

You can guess the outcome. Fiscal restraint had been lifted, for some bizarre reason, and a completely new X-ray building was approved.

— DR. JOHN COCKER

Forsdick the Fearless

As a coroner in rural Saskatchewan, I had a close working relationship with the Royal Canadian Mounted Police. And, of course, as the local physician I also had to deal with many of the same distasteful happenings in the community — beatings, accidents, rapes, et cetera — as the Mounties.

So I wasn't too pleased when my old friend Sergeant McBain was replaced with a glum, snarly Corporal Forsdick, who seemed to have a perpetual wasp up his ass. He appeared to take as a personal affront my attempts to make nasty situations somewhat more bearable by means of a little levity.

In particular, he was enraged when he learned that I habitually referred to him as Fearless Forsdick, after Fearless Fosdick, a cop in the L'il Abner comic strip.

One night I was awakened from a cozy sleep by a call from the corporal, informing me that none of the RCMP cars would start because of the intense cold. From his accusing tone I immediately started to feel guilty, then realized that it was just his usual technique when dealing with any of the public.

I was tempted to suggest a couple of hot water bottles and a blanket for the car and two aspirins and a shot of rye for himself, but fortunately thought better of it. In the process of mulling this over I fell asleep, only to be awakened by a bellow informing me that as coroner I'd have to visit the scene of a death and must pick him up on the way.

It turned out that while I'd fallen asleep on the phone, he'd been explaining all the details of a single-car accident that had caused the death of the driver. He finally realized when I replied with gentle snores instead of the affirmative answers he expected that I wasn't being as alert and attentive as the situation demanded.

I dressed groggily, winced as the bitter cold knifed through my bones on the way to my car, and winced again as I sat on

175

the frozen seat. When I turned on the ignition, the engine groaned but unfortunately started coughing, roaring, and shaking in the alarming way it always did at minus 30 degrees F. The heater squealed and blew out frigid air that somehow managed to cover the previously clear windshield with a pretty but opaque layer of frost.

Fumbling around, I finally found the scraper and laboriously hacked at the now-impervious layer of white, while silently cursing the cold, the night, the winter, the dumb Ford that shouldn't have started, and the heartless corporal.

Next I had to deal with the square tire syndrome caused by the freezing of the tires into a flat-bottomed shape. This was gradually banged back to the circular by a five-minute process of lurching and bumping, which was accentuated by the fact that every spring and shock absorber was frozen into total rigidity.

My cheery, "Lovely night for a death," was greeted by the corporal with a glare that cooled the already icy air. Then, my "It's so cold even the wheels of justice are frozen solid" was met by, *"Drive!"* in a tone that made me decide that silence was safest.

So I drove — for 30 miles straight west, with the sifting, drifting snow trying to lull me to sleep as the north wind whipped it across the highway.

We arrived at the object lesson against driving while drowsy. The car was upright in the ditch, but we could tell from its tracks that it had veered over the edge of the road and the wheels had been cramped over, overcorrecting and causing the car to roll several times. People didn't wear seat belts in those days, and the driver had been thrown around. His head had gotten wedged between the seat and the door while his body had continued to rotate. It was a fate usually reserved for poultry, and so the poor man became an object for the coroner's and Mountie's attention.

After we did all the viewing and measuring and marking down appropriate to our professions, I headed back to Moosomin to send the ambulance to pick up the body while the corporal held the fort. A less dedicated (or rigid) member of the constabulary would have come back with me, as the risk of body snatchers in that place and time and weather seemed

"Pretty good turnout for my first day of practice, eh?"

to me to be sufficiently small to accept. However, I found myself driving back alone with the snow sifting and lulling and drifting and lulling until I'd wake up with a jerk and realize that I, too, had almost suffered that "fate reserved for poultry."

Eventually I reached home, thankfully staggered into my warm house, undressed, even more thankfully climbed into my wife-warmed bed, and fell sound asleep.

I was awakened by the phone. It was about 6:30 a.m. I was still very sleepy but came instantly awake when the words, *"Hanging is too good for the likes of you!"* came screaming down the line.

I suddenly remembered that I'd forgotten to phone the ambulance, thus leaving the corpse and the corporal alone in the gale.

I think it was only the anger mounting and boiling within him when he realized that no ambulance was coming that kept him from freezing that night. Eventually a car came by, and the corporal flagged it down and took it to town.

From then on I was the most law-abiding citizen in town, for I knew I could expect no mercy from this minion of the law. And never again did I dare refer to Forsdick as "Fearless."

— DR. BRADLEY HOUSTON

"I used to feel paranoid until I realized there are those in positions of power who want us to feel paranoid."

Open Your Mouth to Good Nutrition

Health and beauty are important to most of us. We may pause every so often to admire ourselves in the mirror, yet we can't seem to stop questioning ourselves over whether we're doing the right things or not. What can I do to keep my body from rotting right out from underneath me? we ask. How can I become as fit as a fiddle or maybe a bass violin?

Yes, indeed, how can such a miracle of nature be accomplished at least by Friday afternoon? Well, the key to good health is proper nutrition. To start with, a person must have the right amount of chemicals in the body to be considered even marginally alive.

Let's begin our look at nutrition by examining the various compounds that the human body rummages through and eventually uses among the stuff we eat. First of all, we need vitamins, and plenty of them. Vitamins are substances that help promote the activity of other functions in the human body such as scratching and sneezing. They're made out of really weird science junk and can be extracted through an intensive, painstaking, patented process from vitamin-packed items like Kellogg's Corn Flakes, Wheaties, and Cap'n Crunch cereal.

Vitamins can be found in the Yellow Pages, usually under a letter of the alphabet such as vitamin A or vitamin B. You never find vitamins listed under numbers because it's feared that they might be mistaken with highways and people might end up eating our modern road transportation system.

As I said, there are vitamins A, B, C, D, and so on. Scientists don't really know what they do because the government hasn't given them any money to study them or take them out dancing, and so they've made up all kinds of theories and excuses on what they do when they're inside us. (The vitamins, not the scientists.) Until more research is forthcoming, we'll say that vitamins are useful things, like an appendix or my stockbroker.

One vitamin that should be noted is vitamin B. It's important to know about this one because it travels under so many aliases, like thiamine, niacin, riboflavin, Bob Hope, and Eleanor Roosevelt.

Along with vitamins, the human body needs minerals. They're used to build teeth and bones and small houses with bay windows.

Important minerals are:

- Calcium. Necessary for making strong teeth. Can be found in abundance in Milk Duds and cheeseburgers. Calcium cannot be digested properly unless it has sufficient vitamin D, the skin cancer vitamin.
- Iron. Needed for making blood. It's recommended that a person eat an early 1950s automobile every month or so. And don't forget the hubcaps. Chrome helps you keep that gleam in your eye.
- Phosphorus. Another bone-building mineral. Phosphorus comes from safety matches; many professional ball players carry a large supply for consumption during long games.
- Iodine. Keeps the thyroid gland from getting out of control and destroying the country. Comes from salt and flesh wounds.

Then there are the many trace elements that play an important part in magazine sales. These include potassium, magnesium, sulphur, ozone, plastic, dust, and grey poupon.

Next on the menu is protein. Proteins are required for making the cells and tissues of the body, which are the basis for firm muscles, sinews, and bags under the eyes. Proteins are classified as simple, complicated, serious, and frivolous.

The building blocks of proteins are the amino acids. These are organic compounds that are concocted in the body's very own chemical set. Some well-known ones are lysine, leucine, Listerine, Maybelline, and Valvoline.

One article the body definitely needs is oil. Here, some, citing expensive government research published in weighty scientific journals like *The National Enquirer* and *The Globe*, claim that fish oil can be substituted. Italian dressing is fine, too. Italy is an ancient country hundreds of years old and yet people still live there.

The body also must have carbohydrates. These are essential for nourishment and growth and to provide heat and energy. In

"There were no survivors, sir. I'm afraid we'll have to find another test market."

fact, they have substantially more energy than the uppers and steroids that truck drivers often use in training for cross-country marathons.

Carbohydrates can be found hiding in starches, sugars, and cellulose. Cellulose, or "roughage," comes from dead store vegetables that have been preserved somehow by the miracle of refrigeration. Certain silly people in Africa and in the interior of the Amazon mistook this word for cellulite, and thus began the unhealthy habit of cannibalism.

One item you should avoid like the plague, unless you've been inoculated, is cholesterol. Cholesterol is a substance that builds up on the walls of arteries. Don't confuse it with collateral, which is a deposit that collects on the walls of banks.

In order for vitamins and minerals and proteins to do anything, a person needs to drink a lot of water. This is the most important liquid on Earth. Without water we would die. Worse, without water it would be impossible to take a shower or get a decent car wash. Good sources of water are ginger ale, cream soda, 7-Up, and draft beer.

Aside from water and all the rest, let's not forget the role a balanced diet plays in the maintenance of our health. Highly respected nutritionists from such renowned academies as the Ronald McDonald School of Fast Food and the Colonel Sanders Institute of Chicken Toxicology urge the public to eat foods from each of the four basic food groups: (1) the hamburger, (2) the hot dog, (3) the pizza, (4) the taco. Each of these food groups provides something toward the RDA. The RDA has a lot to do with off-track betting and can be found printed on the sides of cereal boxes, bread wrappers and cattle.

Of course, good nutrition is utterly useless unless one keeps physically fit. Several minutes every month should be set aside to exercise. There are aerobic, microbic, and allergenic workouts that can be accomplished with little sweat and even less pain as long as some medicinal beer or wine is consumed along with the activity. You might even consider taking up softball.

So there you have it. Follow the reasonable advice that nutritionists dispense for free and you will be well on your way to living 200 or 300 years. And remember to chew all your food, and don't talk with your mouth full.

— CLYDE JAMES ARAGON

181

Notes on Contributors

Clyde James Aragon is a humour writer who has been published in several national magazines. His main ambition in life is to be taller.

Gillian Arsenault, a family physician in Maple Ridge, British Columbia, is a fan of children, chocolate, and cats, although not necessarily in that order.

Anthony Atkinson is a doctor in Bridgewater, Nova Scotia.

Larry Barza, a family physician from Bradford, Ontario, who is known to the auto racing fraternity as Dr. B., spends his spare time collecting, racing, and repairing cars.

Robert Bisson is a family doctor in Hull, Quebec.

Brian Boyd practises medicine in Toronto, Ontario.

Tony Brilz is a doctor in Calgary, Alberta.

David Brook is a geriatrics consultant in the Department of Family Medicine at the University of British Columbia.

George Burden is a general practitioner from Elmsdale, Nova Scotia. He is a graduate of Dalhousie University and often writes for *Stitches,* the magazine.

Anthony Caspers is a specialist in internal medicine in Guelph, Ontario.

Donald W. Cockcroft is a professor of respiratory medicine at the University of Saskatchewan.

John Cocker, the publisher of *Stitches,* the magazine, is a family doctor in Aurora, Ontario. As well as building and flying his own airplane, he has sailed halfway around the world.

A. J. Cooper is the director of research at the St. Thomas Psychiatric Hospital in Ontario.

Klaus Dittberner is a family physician in Selkirk, Manitoba.

Arnold Dlin is on the staff of the University of British Columbia hospitals.

Danny Dowhal, a product of Toronto's inner city, is a freelance writer, artist, and cartoonist. He trained at Ryerson Polytechnical Institute, where he studied journalism and industrial engineering.

Bill Eaton, an associate professor of family medicine at Memorial University in St. John's Newfoundland, has a special interest in geriatrics and computer applications.

John Egerton has written for journals and newspapers for the past 20 years. He was educated in England but now practises medicine in Friendswood, Texas, with his wife, Judith, who he met in medical school "over a dead body."

Harry Emson is head of pathology at the College of Medicine at the University of Saskatchewan.

Mark Eveson is a psychologist and therapist who specializes in bioenergetic therapy. He believes that professional roles can be taken too seriously.

John Gately practises medicine in Hamilton, Ontario.

M. Gautam is a specialist in child and adolescent psychiatry in Ottawa.

Charles Godfrey is psychiatrist-in-chief at Wellesley Hospital and professor emeritus at the University of Toronto.

Michael Golbey is a family doctor and chairman of the British Columbia Medical Association Computer Committee.

Gordon Griggs is a family physician in Winnipeg, Manitoba.

Peter Hanson, a former family doctor from Newmarket, Ontario, is the author of *The Joy of Stress* and *Stress for Success*. A noted public speaker, his latest publication is *Counterattack*.

Bradley Houston originally hails from Manitoba, where he took his medical training. He practised in Moosomin, Saskatchewan, before moving to his present home in Penticton, British Columbia.

John Kefauver is a prolific fiction writer who has recently published a novel, *The Three-Day Traffic Jam*.

Guy Landry is a doctor in Montreal, Quebec.

Carolyn Lane is a family physician. She is also a clinical lecturer at the University of Calgary.

Burne Larson, a general surgeon, is an assistant professor at the University of Calgary.

Jean Lavallée practises medicine in Quebec City.

John Levine is director of palliative care in Inverness, Nova Scotia.

Alan Lupin is an ear, nose, and throat specialist from Edmonton, Alberta. He is also an adjunct professor of electrical engineering at the University of Alberta and in the Department of Biology at the University of Victoria.

N. K. MacLennan is a doctor in Sydney, Nova Scotia.

Mark Miller, who is qualified in internal medicine, infectious diseases, medical microbiology, epidemiology, and biostatistics, has a secret desire to be a stand-up comic in Las Vegas.

Alistair Munro heads the psychiatry department at Dalhousie University in Halifax. Born and educated in Scotland, he served as psychiatrist-in-chief at Toronto General Hospital in the seventies.

Kenneth Murray, a family doctor in Neil's Harbour, Nova Scotia, is chief of staff at Buchanan Memorial Hospital in that province.

Ewan Porter practises medicine in Owen Sound, Ontario.

Hendrik Reems is a family doctor in Nanaimo, British Columbia.

William Robertson is a physician in Sault Sainte Marie, Ontario.

T. A. Rohland is a doctor in Lower West Pubnico, Nova Scotia.

Jeannie Rosenberg practises medicine in Huntingdon, Quebec.

Barbara Rostron is a family doctor in Calgary, Alberta.

Howard Shiffman is a physician in Calgary, Alberta.

Albert Solway specializes in internal medicine at Toronto Western Hospital.

F. R. Spicer is a doctor in Halifax, Nova Scotia.

Roderick Syme is a vascular surgeon at Queensway-Carleton Hospital in Nepean, Ontario.

Kevin Tompkins is an obstetrician and gynecologist, as well as a part-time bullfighter.

Larry Tritten is a freelance writer whose humorous prose has graced the pages of such magazines as *Playboy, Harper's,* and *Travel and Leisure.*

James Watt practises medicine in Toronto, Ontario.

Ian Wilkinson is a doctor who works as a clinical chemist at the Sunnybrook Health Sciences Centre in Toronto, Ontario.